Abe Wagner

THE
TRANSACTIONAL
MANAGER

How to Solve People Problems
with Transactional Analysis

A SPECTRUM BOOK

Prentice-Hall, Inc., *Englewood Cliffs, N.J. 07632*

Library of Congress Cataloging in Publication Data

Wagner, Abe.
    The transactional manager.

    (A Spectrum Book)
    Bibliography: p.
    Includes index.
    1. Personnel management.   2. Transactional analysis.
3. Interpersonal relations.   I. Title.
HF5549.W258   658.3   80-25490
ISBN 0-13-928192-4
ISBN 0-13-928184-3 (pbk.)

10   9   8   7   6   5   4   3   2

Printed in the United States of America

PRENTICE-HALL INTERNATIONAL, INC., *London*
PRENTICE-HALL OF AUSTRALIA PTY. LIMITED, *Sydney*
PRENTICE-HALL OF CANADA, LTD., *Toronto*
PRENTICE-HALL OF INDIA PRIVATE LIMITED, *New Delhi*
PRENTICE-HALL OF JAPAN, INC., *Tokyo*
PRENTICE-HALL OF SOUTHEAST ASIA PTE. LTD., *Singapore*
WHITEHALL BOOKS LIMITED, *Wellington, New Zealand*

CONTENTS

INTRODUCTION

IX. HOW DO I APPLY TRANSACTIONAL ANALYSIS TO SUPERVISION?

X. WHAT ABOUT MY PERSONAL LIFE?

v

FOREWORD

Some of the transactional analysis theory presented in this book differs from current, "accepted" TA theory, and this is deliberate. I have simplified it, not in disagreement with Berne and later theorists, but to make it more readily useful to people who are unfamiliar with TA. Those readers who would like to know more about traditional TA theory and how it differs from this presentation are invited to consult the books listed in the reference section. Eric Berne himself was a believer in simplicity of theory, and it is in that spirit that I modify the letter of of the law to arrive at something that works efficiently for me and for my clients.

I have found that some of the concepts in TA are cumbersome and confusing for the layperson. This book represents my way of organizing TA concepts and relating them to valuable ideas I have gleaned from other disciplines and from my personal experience as husband, bachelor, father, supervisor, employee, therapist, consultant, friend, and human being. This presentation of TA is designed for people who want to make practical application of these principles at work and in their personal lives.

One major area of difference with many authors in TA is my way of organizing the ego state material. Parenthetically, I feel free to differ with the patriarchs of transactional analysis because I have had practice in differing with those of an even older and more sacred body of knowledge; I have noted discrepancies in the Old Testament. For example, I tend to suspect error in the passage stating that Moses tied his ass to a tree and then walked twenty miles. At any rate, the six funtional entities used in this book have proved to be efficient for introducing a working knowledge of transactional analysis. The use of all ego states is an absolute necessity in childhood because a youngster doesn't have a fully functioning Adult. Grownups who do have a well-informed Adult ego state can learn to use healthier adaptations than those available to a little child. Therefore, I am willing to define certain ego states as "ineffective," even though they were necessary and useful during childhood, and stress the use of those ego states that are more efficient and bring more pleasure in adult life. With an integrated Adult, the positive functions of *all* ego states are carried out by the Nurturing Parent, Adult, and Natural Child.

This book covers theory contributed by many transactional analysts in addition to Eric Berne. I am particularly grateful to Jacqui Schiff and her associates at Cathexis Institute for the material on passivity, to Robert and Mary Goulding for their work on injunctions and redecision, to Stephen Karpman for the Drama Triangle, to John Dusay on egograms, to Taibi Kahler on miniscript, and to Claude Steiner on scripts. Representative works of these authors are listed in the references.

I am especially thankful to Jon Weiss for introducing me to TA. He and Laurie Weiss have taught me so very much. I'm grateful to Donna Jara, who edited this book. I appreciate the thoughtful critiques and continued inspiration I have received from my former associate, Bill Krieger and my partner Glenn Gravelle. Many thanks to "My Lovely Babs," Barbara Rothstein for her encouragement and support.

I am also very grateful to my sons, Doug, Dave, and Dan, for acting as laboratory subjects on whom I could try out my ideas and, especially, for being a constant source of love to me; to my warm and beautiful sister, Rosalie, for being her nurturing self; and to my friends Mort Leiser, Larry Siegel, Jay Gegenberg, and Dave Pells, for their much-appreciated humor. Finally, thanks to the brilliant individuals who have had the foresight to purchase this masterpiece.

INTRODUCTION

The most difficult and lingering problems that arise within organizations do not result from lack of some commodity such as money, machinery, materials, time, ideas, or expertise. If we follow a particular problem back to its roots, we often find that it is actually a "people problem." Somewhere along the line, somebody is angry, resistant, needy, passive, unthinking, obstructive, or in pain. The problem stems from the ineffective way that this individual (or group of individuals) is dealing with feelings, conflicts, and stress. Many organizations try to solve their "people problems" by manipulating commodities (buying a new piece of equipment, putting on an extra shift, adding or dropping a product, and so on) rather than by paying attention to what is going on with the people in the organization. In short, they treat the symptom rather than the cause. If manipulating the commodities happens to make things go better for the people involved, the problem may be solved; if it doesn't, the problem will persist, or worsen, or simply take another form. Clearly it would be more efficient to first investigate the underlying "people problem" before investing time, money, and energy in a "solution" that may or may not bring the desired results.

Many of these "people problems" are quite subtle. Few subordinates are willing to be in open disagreement with their supervisors, and fewer still are overtly obstructive. Instead, people "make mistakes," "have accidents," "misunderstand," "can't," spin their wheels, waste time, get sick, fail to cooperate with each other, and so on. Supervisors often cope with stress in these same ineffective ways, and many are unwilling to confront the inappropriate behaviors of their supervisees.

Most "people problems" are actually "communication problems." Human beings are a sociable species. We tend to cluster together, work together toward certain goals, form attachments to each other, and find our happiness or unhappiness with each other. The basis of all this is communication: we constantly exchange information with each other through words, gestures, body posture, facial expression, tone of voice, and in other ways as well. Before we became civilized, our communication was congruent; that is, we said the same thing through all our avenues of communication. If an uncivilized man was angry, he looked angry, sounded angry, held his body in an angry way, used angry words, and so on. (Watch how a little child communicates anger!) Now that we're civilized and "control ourselves better," our communication is no longer congruent. We may smile when we're sad, use polite words when we're angry, and act confident when we're scared. In other words, we send mixed messages to each other, and this creates problems in communication. We also tend to hide our feelings from ourselves, and this causes us to send mixed messages. *If we don't say it straight, we'll show it crooked.* Some part of us always manages to send the real message, no matter how carefully we control ourselves.

Obviously an organization would break down if everybody communicated as a little child does: tantrums, rages, tears, unrestrained joy, and insistence on "me first, right now!" Organizations also break down, however, when the feelings and thoughts of the people within those organizations are not expressed openly and the needs and wants of these people are not met. It therefore makes sense for members of organizations and groups—and especially for managers and supervisors—to learn communication skills and learn how to help others communicate effectively.

A major factor underlying the Peter Principle[1] is that people who have excellent technical skills are often expected to have, without training, excellent "people skills." After promotion to a supervisory or managerial position, a good technician often fails because he isn't a "people person." He supervises as he was supervised by his parents, his teachers, and his previous supervisors. Unfortunately, such people are often inadequate models for the would-be supervisor. Many do not have the communication skills required for effective supervision.

Before we begin to discuss these communication skills, it is important to examine the foundations on which they are built and without which they will crumble: sensitivity, respect for all human beings, and willingness to change one's own behavior. The "people skills" described in this book are tools for changing your *own* behavior, not tools for manipulating other people. I do not have any control over your behavior; I cannot make you do anything. If I change my behavior in certain ways, however, I can *invite* you to change yours in response. If my communications are honest, congruent and effective, I will often precipitate changes in my personal relationships, my family, my department, my organization, and even in my community. If I focus on changing myself, on becoming an effective communicator, it is likely I will get the responses I seek.

x

The methods offered in this book are applicable to any situation where people are communicating with each other. Though a specific example may refer to a couple, a family, a group, or a large corporation, the principles illustrated are useful in any setting. In many ways, organizations and groups operate like families, and it is often useful to consider them as families when learning new communications skills. We originally learned to communicate within a family group; it is therefore a useful context in which to learn new ways to communicate and new ways to improve the quality of our own lives.

The Transactional Manager has an exercise booklet to help readers integrate the concepts. In addition, the appendix in this book has been reproduced, titled *People Skills for Managers*. This is a summary of key concepts in the book and serves as a handy reference for employees. Six one-hour audio tapes and six one-hour video tapes by Abe Wagner, recorded with a live audience, are also available. Write or call:

Abe Wagner
4250 S. Olive Street #110
Denver, Colorado 80237
(303) 757-7576

EGO STATES DIAGRAM

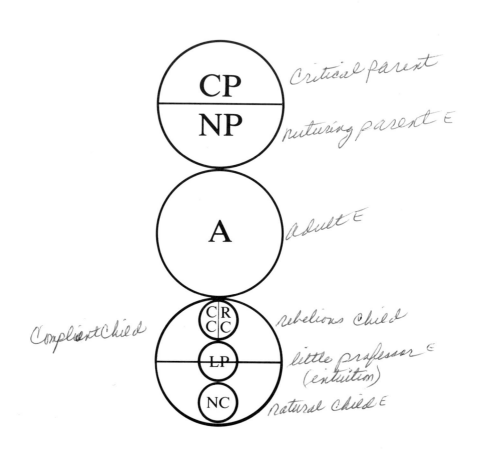

Critical parent

nuturing parent E

adult E

Compliant Child

rebelious child

little professor E
(intuition)

natural child E

E = effective

Chapter I

HOW CAN I MAKE THINGS GO BETTER AROUND HERE?

You are six different people, and so am I. You have six different personalities, and so do your subordinates, your customers, your boss, your spouse, and your children. Right now you are operating within one of those personalities, and at any moment you may activate another one instead. The different parts of your personality have differing opinions, abilities, and ways of communicating with others. This explains why sometimes you are very bright and a few minutes later you forget your best friend's name when introducing him to someone; it also explains why you may be supportive and understanding of your employees on one day, and on another day no one can do anything right as far as you're concerned. It explains why at times you feel self-confident and at other times insecure, and why the instructions you gave last week were followed correctly while the ones you gave this week were not.

Learning about people's shifting personalities can be beneficial for everyone, but it is especially useful for anyone in a managerial or supervisory position. When you become acquainted with your six different personalities, you can more readily use the three effective people in your head while learning to deactivate the ineffective people in your head. You can also learn how to relate to, or stimulate, the healthy rather than the unhealthy parts of others (your boss, subordinates, customers, family members, et cetera). By using your effective personality parts, you greatly increase the probability that the person you're relating to will respond from a healthy part.

One of the hallmarks of a healthy personality part is clear, direct expression of the person's thoughts and feelings—in other words, straight communication. Sooner or later, one way or another, your true thoughts and feelings do get expressed. Some parts of your personality can express them in a positive way, while other parts tend to communicate them in negative, sneaky, or crooked ways.

How do I avoid crooked communication?

If you say it straight, you won't show it crooked. If you express your feelings, thoughts, and desires in a sensitive and effective way, by using your three healthy personalities, you will seldom activate the unhealthy parts of your personality. They will simply not be

1

needed. If you don't express your true needs, thoughts and feelings, however, you will activate the undesired parts. For instance, when you are angry, sad, or fearful, if you do not deal with these feelings effectively (in your head or out loud), you are likely to soon start feeling depressed, hurt, or guilty or to smoke another cigarette, head for the refrigerator, or have another drink. If you are unwilling to let your boss know that you disagree with him, you are likely to sabotage what he asks you to do—without being aware of it—by forgetting to do it, doing it late, doing it wrong, and so on. If you do not ask for what you want or express your feelings directly, you will do so indirectly, and probably in a crooked way. Another means of expressing your feelings in a crooked way is to have psychosomatic problems such as headaches, upset stomach, bowel problems, high blood pressure, et cetera. What it boils down to is, if you have strong wants, needs and feelings that you do not deal with effectively, you are very likely to manifest those and other feelings in ineffective ways. Therefore, the way to avoid crooked communication is to learn how to say it straight in the first place, in a way that gets the job done without stepping on other people's toes. This book will tell you how.

You're talking about me—what about others?

In learning how to express your own needs, wants, thoughts and feelings more effectively, you will also learn how to help others do the same. Paying more attention to your own personality parts will enable you to be more aware of the personality parts of others.

All organizations, regardless of size or purpose, are composed of individual human beings. It would not be possible—or even desirable—for members of an organization to leave all their personal wishes and feelings out in the parking lot, since this would mean leaving their motivation and creativity out there too. Thus, no matter what an organization is doing (manufacturing, teaching, servicing, reporting, selling, building, researching), it is also a social organization, a place where people get together and attempt to gain personal satisfactions from their associations with each other. The most effective managers and supervisors not only accept this fact, they utilize it to the benefit of the organization, its members, and themselves. They realize the importance of their "people skills" and continually seek to improve them.

Fortunately, "people skills" do not have to be learned through trial and error. This book offers a simple and well-tested system for understanding and solving "people problems." Within that system, it offers specific information on such issues as selecting the right person for the job, handling disputes and complaints, firing, training, motivating, dealing with infractions of company policy, designing effective meetings, and "making things go better" in general. The principles will apply to communication and interpersonal relationships in any setting, at home as well as at work. Transactional Analysis provides the framework for the theory in this book, which includes information from Gestalt psychology, communication theory, and small-group theory, as well as my own ideas.

The key to this system is a concept of "OK-ness" that has come from Transactional Analysis (TA). You've probably heard the expression, "I'm OK, you're OK." According to the dictionary, to be OK is to be correct or to be right. The kind of OK-ness we're talking about, however, has nothing to do with being right or correct. It has to do with a human being's inherent worth: "I am a person who is valuable simply because I exist, not because of my race, creed, economic status, physical appearance, intelligence, or any other attribute." To develop effective people skills, we must start with the premise that every human being has intrinsic worth and dignity, that everybody is OK and deserving of consideration.

OK-ness is a state of being, a feeling I have about myself and/or other people. When I feel OK, I like myself and know that I deserve to be counted, to have what I need. How I feel about myself is reflected in how I feel about you and how I invite you to feel about me: when I like myself, I can like you, and I'll let you like me.

My prevailing opinion about the OK-ness of myself and other people is called my "basic position."[2] This is the frame of reference from which I operate most of the time, and it is seen vividly when I'm in a conflict. Clearly, if my basic position is "I'm OK, you're OK," I am more likely to engage in the kinds of cooperative and caring behaviors that are beneficial for me and those around me.

One's own basic position stems from early childhood decisions. From the earliest moment of my existence, I form opinions about myself, other people, and the world. If I am parented in a way that takes care of my needs and wants, I will decide that I am OK and other people are OK. On the other hand, if I am parented in a way that discounts my needs and wants, I am likely to decide that *I* am not OK (if I were, they'd be taking better care of me) or that *they* are not OK (if they were, they'd be taking better care of me). If my needs are

3

discounted at a high enough level, I might even decide that *Nobody* is OK (they're rotten, but it doesn't really matter because I'm worthless anyway). Thus there are four possible basic positions: I'm OK, you're OK; I'm OK, you're not OK; I'm not OK, you're OK; I'm not OK, you're not OK.

My opinion about OK-ness may sometimes vary from situation to situation, but my general pattern of behavior reflects my basic position. If I believe that I'm OK, I'll naturally invite you to treat me that way. I'll select people who treat me with respect. If I decide that I'm basically not-OK, I'll behave in ways that invite you to treat me in that way. I'll select people who will agree with me that I am not OK and who will discount me. If I believe that you're not OK, I'll treat you that way and invite you to provide me with further evidence to support my beliefs about you. In short, I tend to act in a way that perpetuates my basic position. Whatever it is, I'll spend my life trying to prove it. I probably won't be consciously aware that I'm doing this—after all, "That's just the way the world is."

My decision on basic position—along with other decisions about what it's OK (or not-OK) for me to think, feel, and do—determines the kind of life I will lead, the kind of people I will choose to relate to, and the way I will relate to them. These decisions are the basis of my *life script*.[3,4] In order to prove the accuracy of my decisions, I construct a play or story line that will bear them out. I develop a plot and a cast of characters, find suitable people to play the supporting roles, and then proceed to act out my life script. The script encompasses my decisions about whether I will have a short life or a long one, a happy life or a tragic one, and so on.

"Script decisions" determine the patterns by which I will give and get attention and recognition (strokes). If I've decided that I'm OK and you're OK, I will give, accept, and ask for positive strokes. If I've decided that I'm not OK and/or you're not OK, I will give, accept, and actually ask for negative strokes in order to promote this belief. Such stroking patterns help me to continually reaffirm my basic position and the other decisions I made when I was little.

The principles in this book are based on the beliefs that all people have inherent worth and dignity, all people have a right to self-determination, and man is responsible for mankind. (In order to make this last statement acceptable to myself and other feminists, I hasten to amend it and say that *people* are responsible for people. Parenthetically, I'd like to mention that the other day I was walking down the street and saw a man fall into a peoplehole. By the way, I was walking with a young woman in her first year of college—she was a Freshperson. This whole matter of gender can get a little awkward, so I'd like to state that, regardless of the pronouns I use in this book, I'm referring to women *or* men unless the statement refers to a matter that is particularly masculine or feminine. I'm alternating "he" and "she" at random when I want to avoid the use of plural pronouns that would be grammatically incorrect.) To say that people are responsible for people does not mean that one is responsible for other people's thoughts, feelings, or behavior; rather, it means that one is responsible for *taking into consideration* the needs, wants, and feelings of other people. These three premises are the bases of the OK-ness concepts we'll explore in this book.

If I am to develop effective people skills, I need to understand human behavior—especially my own! Here's where Transactional Analysis comes in.

What is Transactional Analysis?

Transactional Analysis is a system for improving communication and for understanding human behavior. TA had its formal beginnings in 1958 when its founder, Eric Berne, M.D.,* began to meet regularly with several other mental health professionals to devise more effective methods for group psychotherapy. Although TA was developed as a form of psychotherapy, TA theory rapidly expanded to become useful in many other areas—education, business, government, industry—wherever people are communicating with each other.

Transactional Analysis is, quite literally, the analysis of transactions: a *transaction* is defined as a *stimulus* plus a *response*. If I say "hello" to you, that's a stimulus; if you smile back, that's a response, and there has been a transaction between us. Not only do transactions take place between people, they also take place inside people's heads—between personality segments called *ego states*.[5] No doubt you have noticed the running commentary that goes on in your head, and how you sometimes seem to be arguing or conversing with yourself, especially when making decisions. For example, at one time

*Dr. Berne wrote a number of books on TA, some of which appear on the reading list in the back of this book.

there were many occasions when people said things I disagreed with and I would have liked to speak up but did not. Instead, I listened to a message in my head that said, "Don't say anything, you'll just cause problems." Realistically, my speaking up would have done no harm, and would have done me some good, yet I listened to that message and kept my mouth shut. When I heard and responded to that message, it was an *internal transaction* between two of my ego states. TA is concerned with this type of transaction as well as with those that take place between individuals.

How is learning about TA going to make me a better manager or supervisor?

As a manager or supervisor, one of your most important jobs is to communicate; that is, to exchange information with other people. You need to convey to your subordinates information about what needs to be done, and whether they're doing it adequately. You need to get information from them, too: If things aren't going well, what's wrong? How can you help? If you and your subordinates were computers, this exchange of information would be relatively simple; with the proper programming, all the information you have could be readily available to them, and vice versa. You are all human beings, however, and as such you are not programmed for instant, complete exchange of information. You are subject to all sorts of rules about what can be said to whom, and how. Furthermore, unlike the computers, feelings are involved in your communications. Computers do not get upset about certain words, orders, or negative feedback; people often do. Computers consistently respond the same way each time they receive a certain stimulus; people often don't. Because people have many different channels of communication, and because they each have somewhat different programming due to individual life experiences, and because they easily and quickly shift from one ego state to another, human communication is complex and fascinating. The most effective managers and supervisors are those who have learned to recognize the functioning of different ego states and respond to them appropriately.

The next chapter will describe the different ego states and how they transact with each other. We will then discuss specific ways to use this and other TA information in your role as manager or supervisor.

Chapter II

WHY ARE PEOPLE SO PREDICTABLE, AND SO UNPREDICTABLE?

When you are dealing with another person, you are actually dealing with a *set* of personalities, rather than with a single personality. Complicating this is the fact that *you* are also operating from a *set* of personalities. Over your lifetime you have developed a set of six distinct personality segments called *ego states*. Each ego state has its own set of beliefs and behaviors, and each interacts differently with other people.

When you were a child, you needed all six of these ego states; each had certain valuable functions in taking care of you and in getting what you wanted. In adult life, however, only three of these ego states are consistently effective in getting what you need and want. For all practical purposes, the other three are ineffective in adulthood; furthermore, if you use them you're likely to have problems in dealing with other people and in feeling OK about yourself.

Many "people problems" stem from an unexpected or unwanted shift from one ego state to another, and from the use of those ego states whose beliefs, behaviors and feelings are inappropriate for the present situation. Therefore, it's important to know what ego state you are in, what ego state the other person is in, and how to switch from one ego state to another.

Are you saying that everybody has six different personalities?

Nearly everyone has these six ego states; however, not everybody uses all six. Some spend most of their time in a few of the ego states and use the rest very little. Others seem "stuck" in one ego state; therefore, you can easily predict their reactions. Certain individuals slip from one to another with such speed and ease that it's hard to tell how they'll react to a given situation. Some people do not seem to have one or more of the ego states available to them.

A well-rounded person will have learned to keep the three ineffective ego states deactivated most of the time and to operate from the three that are more effective in getting needs met and in dealing with others. This person will also know how to invite others to switch to their effective ego states.

7

How do you know that ego states are really there?

Ego states aren't just theoretical concepts, they're "really there" as cell networks in the brain. They have been called "psychic organs" because they exist and function in the brain in much the same way that the heart exists and functions in the chest. The existence of these brain-cell networks was indicated by the neurosurgical studies of Dr. Wilder Penfield and his associates;[6] their functions have been studied by Dr. Eric Berne and dozens of other transactional analysts. When you know what to look for, you can identify ego states and watch them functioning in yourself and in others.

Like bodily organs, ego states have both structure and function; that is, they exist physically and they also do something. Structure and function are important distinctions to transactional analysts, who study ego states from both points of view in the same way a cardiologist studies the heart, for example. The heart has structure (it's an organ with location, shape, parts, etc.) and function (circulation of the blood), and both aspects are of interest to the cardiologist. I can tell that the heart is there, even though I cannot see it, because there is outward manifestation of its presence (heartbeat, pulse, etc.). It is functioning, and I can see what it does, even though I'm not a cardiologist. The same is true of ego states: you don't have to be a psychologist to see that they're in there, ticking away. In this book, we will be dealing with the functions—the outward manifestations—of the ego states.

What can I do if I don't like some part of myself?

You can learn how to avoid energizing the ego states you don't want to use, and how to strengthen the ones you do want to use. All it takes is awareness and practice.

An ego state is activated by a switch in psychic energy: a person can activate a particular network of cells at one moment and then switch to another network a moment later. For example, I can come to work feeling depressed—which means that I'm in a certain one of my ego states—and continue to feel that way until the boss calls me on the phone and asks for some information. To understand and respond to him, I need to switch to another network of cells; as a result, I no longer feel my sad feelings as intensely. This happens because one ego state does most of the thinking, while others do most of the feeling. Folk wisdom has recognized this phenemenon. How often have you heard somebody say, "How about going out tonight?

It'll get your mind off your problems," or "Eat something, you'll feel better," or "The best thing to do is throw yourself into your work!"? These suggestions involve activities that are likely to encourage a change in ego state, so that the individual will tend to move out of an ego state where he is feeling pain, or into one where he will feel pleasure. Clearly, a change in activities can lead to a change in what we are feeling. I'm suggesting that we can also change what we are feeling *without* a change in activities, consciously, whenever we are willing to do so. Once we're aware of our own ego states, we can learn to switch from one to another at will. Through practice, we can learn how to energize the ego state that's most appropriate for what we're doing here and now.

How can I recognize an ego state?

Since ego states have distinctive behavior patterns, they can be identified by a person's words, tone of voice, facial expression, gestures, and body posture. They can also be identified by the response they elicit, because each ego state tends to stimulate certain ego states in other people. If we identify two or three of those factors, we identify the ego state. One factor alone (the words being used, for example) is not conclusive. Later on, I'll be giving more information about identification of certain ego states.

Who are these six people in my head?

There are three main ego states—the Child, the Adult, and the Parent—which can be identified by characteristics typical of actual children, adults, and parents. From a functional point of view, I teach that there are six ego states and that three of them are effective for communication and for getting my needs and wants met. For most practical purposes, the other three ego states are not efficient, not effective, and will not help me to meet my needs. The effective, need-fulfilling ego states are called the Natural Child, the Adult, and the Nurturing Parent. The basically ineffective, need-inhibiting ego states are called the Critical Parent, Rebellious Child, and Compliant Child. These last three ego states had very important and healthy functions in childhood; in adulthood, however, keeping my energy in these ego states can cause interpersonal difficulties and create unpleasant feelings for me.

My Child is me as a little kid, probably somewhere between the ages of two and six years. When I'm in Child, I'm using a network of cells that I developed and used when I was a child; therefore, I have the same needs, wants and feelings that I experienced as a child. For example, as an adult, I sometimes used to feel bad on those rare occasions when a woman I liked didn't want to go out with me. Though I was very "mature" about it and pretended it was OK with me, underneath I felt like the hurt kid who used to take his basketball and go home when he didn't get his way. Now, I am much less likely to feel pain in such a situation. I clearly understand that women who do not want to go out with me are simply suffering from impaired judgment, so now I can turn on my Nurturing Parent ego state and feel sympathetic toward them, instead of sinking into my Child ego state and feeling sad because they don't want to play with me.

When I am in Parent, I am *being* my mother, father, and/or other important people who influenced me in early childhood. When I'm in Parent, I'm not acting as if I were those people, I *am* those people, in that I feel their feelings, believe their beliefs, think and act the same way they did. Regardless of whether I like what they did, I tend to parent other people (my children, my spouse, my employees, my parents, the Child in me) in the same way.

There are three Child ego states: the Natural Child, the Compliant Child, and the Rebellious Child. The Compliant Child and the Rebellious Child are often lumped together and referred to as the Adapted Child, and rightfully so, since they are sometimes two sides of the same coin. A baby learns to adapt to what mother wants by **complying** (that is, by doing whatever Mom indicates that he should do.) For example, the baby may learn not to cry when hungry and instead wait to be fed on Mom's schedule. Later—especially around age two—he learns to adapt to what Mother wants by **rebelling** (by **not** doing what Mom wants, or even by doing the opposite of what she wants). It may seem as if the "rebelling" child is acting autonomously, but actually he is not—his rebellion, just like his compliance, is only in **response** to his mother's wishes. Whether the child complies or rebels, he is **reacting** to what Mother wants, rather than **acting** on what he wants for himself. That's the key difference between the Natural Child and the Adapted Child: the Natural Child is spontaneous and the Adapted Child is under the influence of the Parent (the Parent in my head, or your Parent) and either complies with or defies what the Parent wants. When I'm in Natural Child, I do what I want to do, and I don't do what I don't want to do—I act spontaneously, in accordance with my real feelings, needs, and wants.

Another part of the Child ego state has been named the Little Professor. Not a separate ego state as I see it, the Little Professor is the intuitive part of the personality and is used in conjunction with the three Child ego states.

As I mentioned before, the Adult is the logical, reasonable, rational and unemotional part of my personality. The Adult deals with facts and processes information. There are two Parent ego states, the Nurturing Parent and the Critical Parent, whose functions I have touched on briefly. I'll now describe each of the six ego states in more detail and point out how they can be identified.

Where do they come from and what do they do?

The *Natural Child* is the part of my personality that I'm born with. I'm born with needs, wants, and feelings. A *need* is something I have to have in order to survive; a *want* is not necessary for survival. Wants may represent needs, but they are not needs themselves; e.g., "I need food, and I want a hamburger" or "I need warmth, and I want my blue blanket." Neither hamburgers nor blue blankets are necessary for survival; substitutes will keep me alive just as well. My wants may vary from moment to moment, but my needs remain constant.

In addition to my basic physical needs for air, food, water, warmth, etc., I also have psychological needs. According to Dr. Berne, I need *strokes* in order to survive.[7] A stroke is a unit of attention from another individual ("I need strokes, and I want a compliment!"). Infants must have actual physical strokes in order to survive. Even if all their other needs are taken care of adequately, tiny babies sicken and die if they are not touched and held—a fact that, unfortunately, was demonstrated in old-fashioned orphanages where no one realized the importance of taking time to cuddle and play with the babies. The physiological need for stroking has also been proved in laboratory studies.[8] As adults, we learn to survive on other units of attention such as verbal stroking, but the Natural Child continues to want and enjoy physical strokes. We also have needs for stimulation and structure in our environment. There is a need for sensory stimulation, as evidenced by the discomfort of prisoners in solitary confinement and the hallucinations experienced by subjects in sensory-deprivation experiments. There is also a specific need to structure time, which I'll discuss later.

The need for structure impels us to order the "how's, when's, what's, who's and where's" in our lives. For example, when my boss assigns me an office, tells me what time I'm to be at work and who I'm to report to, my Child feels better because I can order my life around this structure. If the boss does not make the structure clear, my Child will want to push the limits and to test until I find out what the structure is.

When the needs and wants of my Natural Child are met, I respond with a warm feeling. When they are not met, I respond with anger, sadness, and fear. Since these four feelings are the only ones observed naturally in infants, many transactional analysts believe that they are the only "natural" feelings and that all others are "learned." Even these four are natural only if they are based upon what is happening here and now. (If I am angry about something that you did last week, that is no longer a feeling of my Natural Child.)

When I'm in my Natural Child, I tell other people about myself. I tell them what I want and what I need. I want what I want, when I want it. I respond with my here-and-now feelings, which I express through words, tone of voice, facial expression, etc. I can experience joy, act spontaneously, and function creatively. I use words like "Wow!", "I want," "I'm mad," "I'm scared," and "Great!" There is emotion in my voice. I ask for what I want. I am "I-oriented" when I'm in my Natural Child. (Actually, all the Child ego states are "I-oriented," meaning that they all talk about how *I* feel, about what *I* want, whereas the Adult tends to be "it-oriented," dealing with facts and data, and the Parent ego states tend to talk about other people and be "you-oriented.")

The Adapted Child parts of my personality begin to develop during the first year of life. As I've already explained, the Adapted Child is reactive, rather than spontaneous: when I'm in Adapted Child, I respond to Parental influences by doing what others want (from Compliant Child) or by refusing to do what others want (from Rebellious Child). Sometimes what may look like Compliant Child behavior is actually motivated by another ego state. I may choose to do what the Parent in my head wants, or to do what somebody else's Parent wants, because it's also what my Natural Child wants to do. For instance, if you want me to come to the dinner table, I may comply with your wish gladly, from Natural Child, if I am hungry. Even when my Natural Child doesn't want to comply, I may do so because it makes sense. For example, if my boss wants me to be at work at 8 a.m. and my Natural Child would rather sleep until noon, I may decide to comply with his wish because it's to my benefit to keep my job. I have come to this decision after processing data in my Adult and considering what's best for my Natural Child in the long run.

Some people argue that we need to use the Adapted Child ego states as adults because it is healthy to rebel against unreasonable expectations and comply with those that are reasonable. I maintain that, because I must use my Adult to decide whether expectations are reasonable (as in the example above), such adaptations are a function of the Adult rather than of the Adapted Child. Compliance takes place from Compliant Child only if I do something solely because some Parent wants me to do it.

If I am sitting next to a person who looks intriguing and would like to get acquainted with him, and the Parent in my head says, "Don't talk to strangers!", it doesn't make sense to comply with that Parental order unless circumstances indicate that there are other reasons not to talk to him. If there are no other reasons and I nevertheless comply with the Parent message, that is Compliant Child behavior.

I manifest "I'm-not-OK" behavior when I'm in Compliant Child; I comply with the Parent in my head that sends me many "not-OK" messages such as "It's not all right to grow up," "Don't show your feelings," "You're not OK," "Don't get close to other people," et cetera. When I'm in Compliant Child I often experience feelings such as hurt, depression, guilt and confusion. These are not Natural Child feelings; they are *substitute* feelings. (We'll talk more about this later.) I manifest I'm-not-OK behavior through my tone of voice (perhaps whining), facial expression (I might look "hurt"), body posture, gestures, and words like "probably," "maybe," "I'll try," "I can't," "I don't know," "I'm not sure," and so on. Often I will refuse to make eye contact, and sometimes I will speak in a halting or very soft voice. Sometimes when I comply, in my head I really defy: "I'll show you! I'll do it, but I'll make sure it doesn't work." Overtly, I may look Compliant, but covertly I'm Rebellious.

The Rebellious Child also adapts to either the Parent in my head or to your Parent. It adapts by *refusing* to comply with Parental messages, even if compliance would make sense for me. For example, if I'm grossly overweight and am being hassled about this by my Parent and yours, I'm likely to rebel by eating even more, even when I'm not really hungry. Despite the fact that being overweight is detrimental to my health and my appearance, and I know it, my

13

Rebellious Child is saying, "I'm not going to listen to you because you're not OK." The Rebellious Child prefers to react negatively to Parental stimuli, even if this behavior is at variance with the wants of the Natural Child. I can rebel overtly by displaying a negative attitude and stubbornly refusing to comply, or I can rebel more subtly by "forgetting," being confused, procrastinating, making "mistakes," having "accidents," and doing things a little differently from the way people would like me to do them. This ineffective-angry (passive-aggressive) behavior is really saying, "You can't make me!"

Often, defensiveness is a manifestation of the Rebellious Child. When I'm in Rebellious Child, I may sit with arms and legs folded and my back straight—or, I may slouch, sitting on my lower back, and carefully avoid looking at you. I will use gestures that indicate that I'm not going to listen to you, and my words will tend to be short and negative. I may look angry, and that is my predominant feeling.

Since Rebellion must be *experienced* before one can "give up" this behavior, the Rebellious Child is a valuable part of one's personality in childhood. Rebellion is a healthy adaptation in the attempt to become separate from Mother. If I'm allowed to rebel *without* being rejected, I can complete the process of separation. In the face of this rebellion, an understanding parent can say, in a nurturing manner, "I know you don't want to do that, but you have to anyway." Later, when this is appropriate and does not present a danger to the youngster, the parent may say, "I know you don't want to, and you don't have to." Accepting responses of this kind allow the youngster to experience her rebellion and feel powerful as a result. When she feels her own power, she will become separate. If she is not allowed to rebel, or is rejected for rebelling, she will tend to rebel in passive-aggressive, ineffective ways. "Yeah, I'll take out the trash," says the kid who knows that she'll get punished if she doesn't take it out. Then she "accidentally" spills some on the lawn. This is covert rebellion.

During the "recycling years" of the teens, a youngster goes through the same psychological developmental stages as experienced in childhood. Those stages which were originally left unresolved are re-experienced, more strongly, in the teen years. Once again, if parents reject the rebellious behavior the youngster either goes underground (forgets, procrastinates, etc.) or tries harder to rebel overtly. If he is still not allowed to rebel, and therefore does not separate successfully from his parents, his rebellious behavior may continue

14

through adulthood. He now comes to work late, forgets things, starts the opposition movement in the company, and so forth.

It's not too late, however; resolution is still possible in adulthood if the person experiences his rebellion without rejection. He may then feel that he is in control, see the consequences of his rebellious behavior, and recognize that his own needs aren't getting met as a result. It is then likely that he will give up his rebellious behavior. For example, the boss occasionally asks me to work late, and I refuse each time. It's not that I have any real objection to working late, it's just that I don't want to do what she wants me to do. Because I have not yet experienced my rebellion, I feel a strong urge to say "no" to everything she wants from me. If the boss accepts my rebellion and doesn't hassle me with her Parent, then I can experience the natural consequences of my behavior (I don't get the promotion, or the raise I wanted). If I don't like the consequences, I may decide to stop reacting to what she wants and instead go after what I want. Having successfully experienced my rebellion, I no longer have an automatic negative reaction to the wishes of those in authority or to my own Parent messages; I behave more spontaneously and autonomously.

It's clear from this example that the task for those relating with someone in the Rebellious Child ego state (whether that person is one's employee, friend, boss, spouse, or child) is to "set limits" in a firm but caring way and to accept rebellion in situations where that behavior will cause no real damage.

Jon Weiss* has suggested ways of being rebellious in adult life that will help me to experience rebellion without harming myself or others. I can say "no" inside my head (as loudly as I please!), then consider the options and decide whether to comply. I can say "no" out loud and give my reasons, when this makes sense. I can contract with specific people to accept my being oppositional in specific ways; for example, I can make an agreement with you that I'll be late to dinner twice a week. Or, we can agree that I'll immediately say "no" to everything you request. Having already rebelled and gotten that issue out of the way, I will then consider the alternatives and decide what I really want to do (which might even be to say yes). These are rebellious behaviors programmed by the Adult, but they nevertheless

*Jonathan B. Weiss, Ph.D., is a psychotherapist, consultant, Clinical Teaching Member of the International Transactional Analysis Association, and Clinical Director of the Rocky Mountain Transactional Analysis Institute in Denver, Colorado.

allow me to experience my power and to give up my rebellion, having finally resolved the issue of separation from your Parent and mine.

The Little Professor is the intelligence of the Child ego state. It makes the very important decisions about what I can and can't "get away with." The Little Professor is intuitive, manipulative, creative and clever; it's the source of my "gut feelings." I describe it as an antenna that tunes in to subtle messages from other people, messages I may not have perceived with my Adult and may not be able to explain how I received. The Little Professor can be used in conjunction with my Natural Child when I'm being creative or clever, or wanting to get out of a difficult situation through guile. It can be used with my Compliant Child to figure out how to get along under the restrictions of Parental messages, and it can be used with my Rebellious Child to figure out loopholes, evasive tactics, and clever, sneaky ways of avoiding compliance and responsible actions.

My Little Professor tunes in to people and really senses who they are, even though they think that they are hiding their feelings. It's the part of me that is a quick wit and intuitively does and says the right thing at the right time. I'm reminded of the story of the big Texan who goes up to a rather puny-looking employee in the produce department of a supermarket and says, "Son, I'd like to have a half a head of lettuce." The produce man replies in a halting, rather shy way, "Sir, we're not allowed to cut..." "Boy," the Texan interrupts, "I said I want a half a head of lettuce, and I'm not going to say it again!" The employee says, in a timid voice, "I'll go and ask the manager, and if he says it's OK, it's sure OK with me, sir!" With this, the small man marches into the manager's office, not realizing that the big Texan is following him, step for step. "Sir, there's the meanest son of a bitch out there, getting all over my back for a half a head of lettuce." Out of the corner of his eye he sees the Texan. While his Natural Child feels scared, his Little Professor is saying, "And this gentleman would like the other half." The next day, the manager calls him in, praises his clever handling of the customer, and offers him a manager's job in Minneapolis, Minnesota. He replies, in a disgusted whine, "Minneapolis, Minnesota? I don't want to go to Minneapolis, Minnesota!" "Why not? You'll be manager of the store, you'll make more money, and Minneapolis is a wonderful place to live." "Wonderful place to live?" replies the candid young man. "Why, all they have in Minneapolis is hockey players and prostitutes." The manager responded angrily, "Just one damn minute, *my wife* is from

Minneapolis." Again, the produce man's frightened Natural Child turned to his Little Professor for help, who asked, "Oh really, sir? What position did she play?"

Jacqui Schiff of Cathexis Institute has made the point that the Adult and the Parent are in the service of the Child.[9] Essentially, she has said that people turn on their Adults to make sense out of the world for the Child and turn on their Parents to protect and nurture the Child. I believe that the only reason people turn on Compliant Child, Rebellious Child, or Critical Parent is because they have discounted their Natural Child. This means that, when they have unexpressed feelings or unmet needs, they turn to old, familiar ways of dealing with the problem, even though those ways are ineffective. They try to meet their wants or express their feelings by reverting to Adapted Child (getting depressed, feeling hurt, overeating, smoking, withdrawing) or to Critical Parent (finding fault, accusing, being sarcastic, etc.). A mother who felt very scared about her son's running away from home expressed that feeling to me with a tear in her eye. She said, "When I get a hold of him, I'll tell him how angry I am at him for doing this to me!" In essence, she was unwilling to express her Natural Child fear and Nurturing Parent concern to him and instead was willing to express her anger from Critical Parent. This is an old, familiar behavior pattern for her that was often modeled by her father. In times of stress, she tends to fall back on this behavior, even though it has not been very effective in dealing with her problems.

The Adult ego state begins development somewhere in the first year of life and can be used effectively by about age 30 months. The Adult continues to develop throughout life. It is logical, reasonable, rational, and unemotional; it does not have feelings such as anger, joy, sadness, fear and frustration. However, I can have my psychic energy in my Adult and simultaneously experience feelings in another ego state.

The Adult is the sender and receiver of factual information. The body posture of the Adult is often erect but relaxed. A person in Adult usually sits up straight, with the head either level or tilted slightly to one side. Adult words are sometimes polysyllabic; they are usually descriptive rather than opinionated. The Adult does not exaggerate or belittle—its descriptions tend to be accurate. It stores data, computes probabilities, and processes information. When I'm in my Adult, my facial expression usually does not convey any emotion: I "look like I'm thinking," which I am. My voice is fairly even in volume and pitch.

A key goal in TA is to put your Adult in charge of your personality (your Child and Parent). This is called "keeping your Adult in the executive position." When my Adult is in the executive position, this means that I think before I act and am likely to be effective. It does NOT mean that I function like a computer and do not feel. A mature individual in good emotional health displays a strong Natural Child and Nurturing Parent as well as exhibiting a well-informed Adult who calls the signals.

A sound decision-making principle involves the use of your Adult: Do what you *want* if it makes sense to your Adult, and do what you *should* if that makes sense. If you do only what your Child wants to do, you'll often do things you're sorry for later on. If you do exclusively what your Parent says you should, there's nothing in it for your Child. Furthermore, if you leave Parental directives unexamined and do only the "right" thing, it's hard to learn anything new or make changes for the better. Sometimes your Adult and Child need to compromise: if you always do what's "sensible" according to your Adult, you don't have any fun! I'm reminded of Tommy, an eleven-year-old boy who used his Adult (and perhaps his Little Professor) to decide what made sense for him. Mother walked into Tommy's bedroom and surprised him while he was masturbating. She said, from Critical Parent, "Tommy, you mustn't ever do that! If you keep on doing that, you'll go blind!" Tommy replied, "Can I just do it until I have to wear glasses?" Tommy was willing to compromise.

The Parent ego state begins to form somewhere around one year of age and is completely formed at age eight or nine, though we can add more Parent messages at any age. The Parent is patterned after our actual parents or caretakers and is also influenced by other people who played significant roles in our childhood years. It is like a collection of videotape recordings of the people who parented us and were important to us in early life. The Parent also incorporates childhood decisions that we make; e.g., if I decide that women can't be trusted, my Parent will incorporate that belief and periodically will tell it to my Child. We continually re-play these Parent recordings and, in essence, become our own mothers and fathers, even if we didn't like the way they were and the things they said. The Parent is the place where we house our value systems—the shoulds, the should nots, the rights, the wrongs, the goods, the bads, the musts, and the mustn'ts.

18

Within the Parent are two functional ego states, the Nurturing Parent and the Critical Parent. The Nurturing Parent is the part of my personality that is understanding and caring about other people. It sends a "you're OK" message. This part of my personality is very capable of setting limits in a reasonable, firm and effective way. It will tell me, and other people, which behaviors are OK and which are not OK, but it will do so in such a manner that the other person is not invited to feel "put down." When I'm in my Nurturing Parent, my tone of voice is often soothing, and my gestures are soft and caring. My words indicate understanding and yet may firmly set limits. I tend to give "do" messages instead of "don't" messages; e.g., "Walk and you'll be safe" vs. "Don't run!" ("Don't" messages tell you what to stop doing but not what to do instead.) My Nurturing Parent is supportive of you and supportive of me.

The message of the Critical Parent is that *you are not OK*. This message is sent by tone of voice, facial expression and gestures as well as by words. You will note that the Critical Parent is not saying that your *behavior* is not OK (which is what the Nurturing Parent may say); instead, it says that *you* are not OK. It invites you to feel not-OK about yourself. My own Critical Parent also tells me that *I'm* not OK.

The Critical Parent tends to use "don't" instead of "do," uses sarcasm, tells people what's wrong with them, and tends to exaggerate and generalize. It deals with opinions rather than fact. The Critical Parent puts down my Child ego state and yours. Being angry from Parent is *you*-oriented ("You're always late!"). Many people have experienced Critical Parent anger and have decided that anger is bad, when the real culprit is the ego state from which the anger is being expressed, not the emotion itself.

When I'm in Critical Parent, my voice tends to be louder and harsher, and I often gesture with my finger pointed at you. My head may be tilted back, so that my nose is up and my eyes are looking down on people, and I'll use words like "should," "shouldn't," "right," "wrong," "good," "bad," "always," and "never." Use of these words does not always indicate Critical Parent; they can be Nurturing. Again, *two or more* signs are necessary for determination of an ego state. If I say, in a caring and concerned tone, "You really shouldn't smoke so much," that's not a Critical Parent statement.

The Critical Parent also has a tendency to Rescue.[10] To Rescue, with a capital "R," means to do for people something they are capable of doing for themselves and, in the process, to put them down (discount them). Often, you put yourself down when you Rescue: you discount your own needs, wants or feelings. A Rescuer may appear to be in Nurturing Parent because he's "doing good" for someone; however, because of the accompanying "you're-not-OK" message, he's really in Critical Parent. For example, if I "help" my son with his homework by doing it for him, I'm Rescuing him (doing something he's capable of doing for himself) and, in the process, agreeing that he is not OK (implying that he's incapable of doing it himself). On the other hand, if my son is doing his homework and asks me for help in understanding a concept that is new to him, and I'm willing to explain it, that is not a Rescue; no discount is involved. If I'm drowning in the ocean and call for help, and you pull me out, that's a *real* rescue (small "r"!)—you have done for me something that I cannot do for myself, in response to my request. Again, no discount is involved, and we're both OK. It's fine to do things for others, as long as no one is put down in the process.

Some Rescues look pretty good on the surface—they're "nice" things to do for people—but, because of the discount, somebody ends up feeling bad (the Rescuer, the person who was Rescued, or both). Even the most benign Rescues tend to deny others an opportunity for growth and can lead to emotional games (a subject we'll be discussing later).

As a reformed Rescuer, I've noted in myself and others an interesting phenomenon: the Rescuer often feels rejected. As a child I didn't get certain wants and needs met. I decided that if I did things for others, they would really appreciate and accept me. I had a father who modeled being a Rescuer. (This is often true of Rescuers: somebody showed them how.) I married someone who seemed to need Rescuing. Despite the fact that I was such a good, helpful person, I was neither appreciated nor accepted, so I played the game of "After all I've done for you, look what thanks I get." I ended up feeling lonely and rejected, the way I started out—a Victim. As is usual in Rescuing, the sequence of roles I played was Victim to Rescuer to Victim again. We'll talk more about this process when we discuss the Karpman Drama Triangle.

The three effective ego states tend to stimulate effective ego states in others. Again, they do not always succeed in doing so (thank God and Her wondrous ways!) because *the person responding is in charge of the response.* For example, I may choose to respond to a person who is in Rebellious Child by being understanding (from my Nurturing Parent). Generally speaking, however, Rebellious Child and Compliant Child stimulate Critical Parent (though Compliant Child *may* stimulate a Nurturing Parent response). Critical Parent stimulates a Rebellious Child or Compliant Child response. (Clearly, a supervisor who comes on as Critical Parent is inviting problems!)

OK-ness stimulates OK-ness, and not-OK-ness stimulates not-OK-ness. For example, if a person accuses you of something and you respond by defending yourself or denying the accusation, you are inadvertently sending stimuli to a need-inhibiting ego state in him. You are talking back to the same ego state (Critical Parent) that accused you; therefore, the person will tend to stay in Critical Parent and the conversation will be likely to continue from the same ego states. On the other hand, if you were to spend a moment paraphrasing what he says (Adult behavior) and being understanding of his comment (from Nurturing Parent), this would invite him to switch to a healthier ego state.

A person who relates well with others uses the three effective ego states most of the time in her day-to-day interactions with family, friends, and colleagues. She has learned how to activate her brain-cell networks that are effective in transacting with others and in taking care of herself, as well as how to deactivate her ineffective networks. She has also learned how to send stimuli to the same need-fulfilling ego states in other people and how to avoid sending stimuli to their need-inhibiting ego states. She has reached a key goal in transactional analysis: she stimulates OK-ness by fostering transactions among the three effective ego states.

How do I foster OK transactions?

I've already defined a *transaction* as a stimulus and its response, taking place between ego states, internally or externally. A goal in transactional analysis is to achieve OK, complementary transactions; that is, transactions between Natural Child and Natural Child, Nurturing Parent and Natural Child, Adult and Adult, Nurturing Parent and Nurturing Parent.

There are four types of transactions, two occurring on an open level and two carrying hidden psychological messages. The open transactions are either *complementary* or *crossed;* the others are *ulterior* transactions and what I define as *transference* transactions.

21

Eric Berne stated rules of communication for the first three, and I'll give mine for the fourth: In a complementary transaction, communication can continue indefinitely. In a crossed transaction, communication is interrupted. In an ulterior transaction, communication takes place on both a social (open) and a psychological (hidden) level; the response is to the psychological-level message. In a transference transaction, communication takes place on a social and a psychological level because the receiver responds to an *imaginary* psychological message. In other words, the message is sent on a social level but is distorted by the receiver and responded to as if it contained a psychological-level message.

Transactions that take place between the more effective ego states I call "OK transactions," and transactions involving one or more of the less effective ego states I call "not-OK transactions." In an OK transaction, I'm OK and so are you: the needs, wants, thoughts, opinions, and feelings of both of us are taken into account.

Complementary transactions take place between *any two* ego states. The ego state that is stimulated is the one that responds. When a complementary transaction is diagrammed, the vectors (arrows) representing the stimulus and the response are parallel:

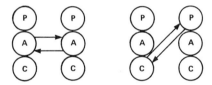

There are OK and not-OK complementary transactions. The OK ones involve the three effective ego states (NC-NC, NC-NP, A-A, NP-NP). Note that it is rare to have an Adult stimulus directed to any ego state except Adult. In a not-OK complementary transaction, the stimulus, the response, or both, come from an ineffective ego state (CC-NP, CC-CP, CC-CC, RC-CP, RC-RC, NP-RC, CP-CP). These transactions are not OK because one (or both) of the ego states is saying that I'm not OK, you're not OK, or others are not OK. Here's a set of not-OK transactions between Compliant Child and Nurturing Parent:

CC: "I can't do anything right!" ("I'm not OK.")

NP: "Of course you can, dear!" ("Yes you are.")

CC: "No, I always mess things up." ("No, I'm not!")

NP: "But you always try your best..." (et cetera)

Another not-OK complementary transaction takes place between Critical Parent and Critical Parent:

CP: "Joe's doing a lousy job." (Joe is not OK.)

CP: "He sure is. He's always screwing up." (He's not OK.)

Note that in this transaction two people are talking in an opinionated way about a third party. If we could hear their voices as well as see their words, it would be clear that they are saying that *Joe* is not OK. If they were having a factual discussion about Joe's *performance,* it would be an Adult-to-Adult transaction.

Here are some OK complementary transactions:

NP: "Joe is sure a nice guy."

NP: "He sure is!"

NC: "Will you help me?"

NP: "I'll be glad to."

NP: "You look tired—let me rub your back."

NC: "Thanks, that would feel great!"

NC: "I like you."

NC: "Gee, thanks!"

A: "What time is it?"

A: "It's 3:27."

As long as transactions remain complementary, the subject of the conversation does not change. For example, in this exchange

CP: "Shut up!"

RC: "I don't have to!"

CP: "Yes, you do!"

RC: "No, I don't!"

only two ego states are involved, the transactions have remained complementary, and the subject has remained the same, even though the Critical Parent and the Rebellious Child are in disagreement about the subject. This sort of exchange can go on indefinitely, until somebody decides to cross a transaction and change the subject, and it will tend to get louder as it continues. This is clearly a not-OK set of complementary transactions: two ineffective ego states are involved, and the disagreement is not being resolved.

People sometimes confuse complementary transactions with the giving or receiving of compliments. Though a compliment can be given and received in a complementary transaction, most often such transactions have nothing to do with compliments (as in the example above). A complement is "something that completes a whole or makes perfect by supplying what is needed" (Webster's New World Dictionary). Complementary transactions are "complete" in that they "complete a circuit"—the response returns to the ego state that sent the stimulus.

In fostering OK transactions, we are concerned with stroking an OK ego state which we believe will invite and reinforce OK behavior. If we stroke a not-OK ego state, that invites a not-OK response. For example, if a person is late to work and we scold him from Critical Parent, we are talking to (stroking) his Rebellious Child; therefore, the rebellious behavior is likely to continue in one form or another. On the other hand, if we set limits in a reasonable and firm way, from Nurturing Parent, we are talking to his Natural Child and more likely to be heard, rather than to invite continued rebellion. Note the difference between:

CP: "Sam, you'd better be on time or you're gonna lose your job!" (said harshly)

and

NP: "Sam, it's important for you to be on time." (said in a soft, reasonable tone of voice) "Please make every effort to do this."

I hasten to mention that if the only time I stroke Sam is when he goofs up, it's likely that he'll continue to goof up. Even if I confront him from Nurturing Parent, it is unlikely that his Natural Child or Adult will hear my confrontation. If Sam is stroked only for not-OK behavior, he is likely to be defensive and respond from Rebellious Child, regardless of the source of the stimulus. Remember, what you stroke is what you get! If you want OK behavior, stroke OK ego states.

Certain ego states tend to stimulate certain other ego states: Nurturing Parent tends to stimulate Natural Child, for example. It may stimulate Compliant Child. Or, if it's directed at somebody else's Parent, it's likely to stimulate Nurturing Parent, as in the exchange about Joe being a "nice guy." The way you know where a stimulus is being directed is by "listening for the melody." Is it a little kid talking to another little kid? Is it a little kid talking to a parent? Is it a parent talking to another parent? Is it a parent talking to a little kid? Or, is it an adult talking to another adult? Very often, it becomes clear where the stimulus was sent only after hearing the response. For example, one person asks, "Will you help me with this?" and the other responds (in a very soothing voice), "Sure, I'd be glad to!" Although the stimulus appeared to be from one Adult to another, it received a Nurturing Parent response; therefore, it's likely that the stimulus actually came from a Child ego state.

Natural Child tends to stimulate Natural Child or Nurturing Parent. Adult tends to stimulate Adult. In general, the effective ego states have a strong tendency to stimulate the effective ego states of others. Likewise, the ineffective ego states are very likely to stimulate an ineffective ego state in someone else: Critical Parent tends to stimulate Compliant Child or Rebellious Child; Rebellious Child tends to stimulate Critical Parent; Compliant Child tends to stimulate Nurturing Parent or Critical Parent; two Critical Parents can get together about a third party or the world in general, and so on.

It is important to be aware that *the person receiving a stimulus is in charge of the response and has control over it.* Though certain ego states do *tend* to stimulate certain ego states in others, and often succeed in doing so, a stimulated ego state is under no obligation to respond. The other person can choose whether to respond from the ego state that was stimulated.

One of your ego states tends to stimulate one of mine because I have developed certain patterns of response: I have established "wiring" in my brain, so that I don't *have* to think about how to respond to every stimulus I receive. I have some fairly standard responses to certain stimuli, and I can just "run on automatic" if I want to, thus saving time and energy. My standard responses may or may not be effective, however: some work well for me, and some don't. With my Adult calling the shots, I can choose to examine the stimuli I receive and decide whether my usual pattern will be effective for me under these circumstances. Therefore, if you send me a message from your Critical Parent, which will probably stimulate my Compliant Child or my Rebellious Child, *I* am in charge of whether I respond from the stimulated ego state or choose some other response. Also, it's possible that your message from Critical Parent will *not* stimulate my Adapted Child. Maybe I hear the information, from my Adult, and don't even notice your facial expression and tone of voice. Or maybe

I'm preoccupied and am just not paying attention. Possibly I misinterpret your message. At any rate, your Critical Parent only *tends* to stimulate my Adapted Child; if it does, there is still no necessity for me to respond from that ego state. As we will see, I am free to cross the transaction by responding from the ego state of my choice.

In a *crossed transaction,* communication takes place between three or four ego states. A crossed transaction usually interrupts communication; that is, either the subject changes or the exchange stops. When I cross a transaction, I am stroking (sending a stimulus to) a different ego state from the one that related to me. The vectors are not parallel and are usually crossed on the diagram:

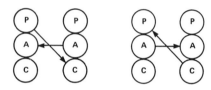

There are OK and not-OK crossed transactions. For example, it's OK (and advisable) to deliberately cross transactions when somebody is in Rebellious Child, Compliant Child, or Critical Parent. Fortunately, if I perceive you to be in an ineffective ego state, I can attempt to elicit one of your effective ego states instead. In order to do this, I must cross the transaction. (For example, if you have sent me a stimulus from your Critical Parent, I can choose to cross the transaction by responding from my Adult to yours.) The goal of crossing the transaction from an effective ego state is to arrive at OK, complementary transactions so that factual information can be exchanged, work can get done, positive strokes can be exchanged, conflicts can be resolved, feelings can be expressed in a constructive way, and so on. OK, complementary transactions help us to communicate clearly and get things done effectively, and the crossed transaction is a means of achieving complementary transactions.

A rule of thumb that I have found helpful is this: when other people are in Child, you can cross from your Child; when others are in Parent you can cross from your Parent. By this, I mean that you can divert their Compliant Child or Rebellious Child with a stimulus from your Natural Child to theirs, and their Parent by a stimulus from your Nurturing Parent to their Natural Child. When their Natural Child is heard and understood, this invites them to switch to Nurturing Parent, Adult, or Natural Child. If they do so, your goal of creating OK, complementary transactions is achieved.

Theoretically, you can cross a transaction from any effective ego state and increase the likelihood that an effective ego state in the other person will respond. I have found from experience, however, that they do not all work equally well in every situation. In addition to the aforementioned "rule of thumb," there are other options. When dealing with a Critical Parent, for example, you can cross the transaction from Adult, or you can start by being understanding (from Nurturing Parent) and then switch to Adult. Your task is to stimulate the other person's Adult to *think* in response to you. I have found that if I respond to a Critical Parent from Natural Child, the other person has a tendency to stay in Critical Parent. The Adult is a second option for crossing transactions initiated by a Compliant Child. I have found that responding from Nurturing Parent invites the other person to stay in Compliant Child. The only ego state that consistently does not respond well to Adult is the Rebellious Child, and in this case a Nurturing Parent response is a second option in addition to one from Natural Child.

Here are some examples of effectively crossed transactions:

CP: (angrily) You blew it again! Now we've lost the Jones account!

NP: (sympathetically) I can understand why you're upset. That was an important account.

A: Would you like to know the reasons they gave for switching to our competitors?

CC: (whining) I'll never be able to get this report done on time!

NC: (grinning) Well, then, we might as well have a coffee break!

(or)

A: What do you need in order to get it finished?

27

Another important rule of thumb is this: When the stimulus involves anger or criticism, respond first from your Nurturing Parent ego state. In Nurturing Parent, you can be understanding and can communicate that you acknowledge the other person's feelings or point of view. Specifically, when a person is expressing anger from Natural Child, Critical Parent or Rebellious Child, and is stating an oppositional or critical point of view, it is effective to respond from Nurturing Parent. This lets her Child know that you care, or at least understand, and this increases the chance that she will be receptive to resolving the issue or ending the anger. She will be likely to switch to Nurturing Parent, Adult, or Natural Child. Conversely, if you don't acknowledge her feelings or opinions, or simply counter with your point of view, it's likely that she will continue to feel angry and repeat her opinions in a different way. To acknowledge does not necessarily mean to agree. It is often effective to simply re-state the other person's feelings or ideas in your own words, thus showing that you hear what that person is attempting to communicate. (This idea will be dealt with more fully in Chapter VII.) After the initial response from Nurturing Parent, you can then switch to your Adult and stroke the Adult of the other person.

Understanding is powerful. If you *understand* the other person's feelings (whether or not you believe those feelings are justified or appropriate) and if you understand the other person's point of view (whether or not you agree with it) and if you communicate your understanding, that person will be much more likely to accept your invitation into OK, complementary transactions. While there are no guarantees that other people will respond to your invitations, if you stay in an appropriate ego state and avoid stroking their less-effective ego states it's likely that they will *want* to switch in order to uncross the transactions and continue communicating with you. If they don't switch, you can choose to stop transacting at that time, without rejecting the person. Often they'll be willing to switch ego states later.

If you are successful in crossing transactions by responding from one of your OK ego states, you'll end up with OK, complementary transactions. Crossed transactions can also be destructive, when people respond to Adult, Natural Child, or Nurturing Parent stimuli from Critical Parent, Rebellious Child, or Compliant Child. A typical not-OK cross results when an Adult request for information ("Is dinner ready yet?") is misinterpreted as impatient whining from

Adapted Child or nagging from Critical Parent and is responded to in that way. Obviously, stimuli are not always received in the spirit in which they are sent! Why not? A major reason is the phenomenon of *transference*, in which a person transfers old feelings from the past into the present. I call it a *transference transaction* when I cross a transaction by responding to you *as if* you were somebody else (Mother, Father, etc.) and transferring the same old feelings I had with them into the present-day situation with you. In this type of crossed transaction, the receiver of the stimulus distorts and misinterprets it.

A typical transference transaction occurs when an employer (from Adult) asks her employee to come into her office to chat for a minute. Though the boss only wants to ask an Adult question, the employee misperceives her as coming from Critical Parent; therefore, he walks into her office either very frightened (Compliant Child) or loaded for bear (Rebellious Child). He expects the boss to do something that she has no intention of doing, or he responds to her as if she is criticizing him when she is not. He is bringing in old feelings from the past, feelings that help him to distort his perception of what's going on here and now. Therefore, he may also overreact to the mildest criticism or direction from his boss. He is relating to her *as if* she were some authority figure from his past (father, mother, teacher etc.) and thus is not responding appropriately in his transactions with her. So if she asks: "Has the Smith proposal gone out yet?" (a simple request for information, from Adult), the employee may interpret this as nagging ("*When* are you ever going to get that proposal out?") or criticism ("Why in the world don't you have that proposal out yet?" or "You can't be trusted to do what you're supposed to do, so I'm checking up on you."). Such misperceptions are the result of *contamination* of the employee's Adult ego state. The Adult is contaminated when it contains Child or Parent beliefs that are accepted as fact. Contaminations are diagrammed like this:

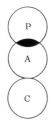

The Adult
contaminated
by the Parent

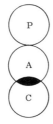

The Adult
contaminated
by the Child

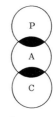

The Adult
contaminated by the
Parent and Child

If an Adult stimulus reaches a contaminated area in the receiver's Adult, then the response is likely to be from the source of the contamination rather than from the Adult ego state itself. Most individuals have at least some areas of contamination in their Adult ego states. Therefore, transference transactions are very common and, as you might imagine, cause a great deal of trouble in interpersonal relationships. When I become aware that I am distorting reality with transference transactions, that's a big step toward my ability to respond appropriately to your stimuli and keep our transactions OK.

Contaminations often cloud a person's ability to see what's really going on and to objectively evaluate a person or problem. For example, a person who has had negative experiences with a member or members of a minority group can decide that all persons belonging to that group are the same way. Prejudice is a Parent contamination of the Adult. A Child contamination of the Adult often has to do with unresolved feelings. If I have unresolved feelings of anger or fear toward one or both of my parents, for example, those feelings tend to interfere with my ability to see reality. It is as if I have a very sensitive spot in my psyche that, when exposed, tends to overreact to or distort what is going on. If I found my father to be very domineering and was either rebellious or compliant with him as a child, I may tend to have these same feelings of anger or fear with anyone who has authority over me now. Consequently, in many situations—at work, or even with my spouse—I tend to distort what people are saying to me, because I see them as if they were my mother or my father and tend to respond with the same feelings I had about my parents when I was little. Phobias—unnatural, irrational fears—are essentially a Child contamination of the Adult. Delusions and hallucinations represent severe contaminations of the Adult ego state.

Transactional analysis offers a number of ways to decontaminate the Adult. Some occur in therapy and some, as you will see, can be do-it-yourself projects.

Berne stated that *ulterior transactions* take place on both the social and the psychological level; that is, on both an open and a hidden level. While communication takes place on both levels, the actual response is to the psychological message. A misleading stimulus is sent. For example, when Mother knows that her son is getting into the cookie jar in the next room and hollers to him, "What are you doing in there, Tommy?" she is asking a question that appears to be Adult-to-Adult, but at the same time, from her Parent to his Child, is inviting Tommy to lie to her. Tommy responds by saying "Nothing!", which on the surface appears to be an Adult-to-Adult response but on the psychological level is a response from his Child to her Parent. (The ulterior transaction often signals the beginning of a psychological game such as Now I've Got You/Kick Me, as we will see in Chapter V.) Mother walks in and "catches" Tommy—and gets angry because he lied to her. Tommy has arranged to "get kicked." This destructive ulterior transaction ended in a game. Some are more benign; for example, the transaction that results when a man invites a woman to his apartment "to listen to music." On the surface is an Adult-to-Adult stimulus (an invitation to listen to music), and underneath the surface is a Child-to-Child stimulus (a "Let's get sexy" message). The woman responds from her Adult by saying, "OK, that sounds interesting," while underneath, from her Child, the response is, "I'm interested!" These ulterior messages are sent by gestures, facial expressions, circumstances, timing, et cetera. Even this socially acceptable kind of ulterior transaction can lead to problems, as the psychological messages can later be denied ("I never said anything of the sort!"). Any ulterior transaction can be the start of a psychological game. By and large, ulterior transactions are ineffective and invite people to relate with each other in destructive ways.

I can discourage ulterior transactions by being willing to express my feelings openly, by asking for what I want, and by responding openly and honestly to ulterior stimuli sent by others. By so doing I can stimulate OK, complementary transactions and authentic communication.

How can I change my own ego states?

A switch in ego states can often be made simply by *deciding* to energize another ego state. That decision is not made, however, unless there is some awareness that switching would be desirable. Such awareness is possible because, even though we may have most of our energy invested in one ego state, others may be somewhat active at the same time. For example, even when I am in Natural Child, my Nurturing Parent and Adult may be watching, ready to take over if needed. When I switch ego states, I move from one state of existence to another; that is, I can feel good feelings instead of bad feelings, or think instead of feel, at a given moment. The ability to switch ego states at will is of value to everyone. For example, how many salespeople, after not making the last sale, get into a negative frame of mind and proceed to do badly in their next encounters with customers? The reason they feel bad is that they get into, or remain in, Adapted Child or Critical Parent. When they learn to switch ego states at will, they can be effective with their next clients despite their earlier disappointments.

My goal in switching ego states is to get into Natural Child, Adult, or Nurturing Parent, whichever is appropriate for the situation. How I get to which ego state is dependent on personal preference. Some people find that nurturing themselves works well. Others prefer to get logical as a means of switching into the desired ego state. In order to switch ego states at will, it is necessary to think. You may wish to identify the ego state you're in, or just to realize that you are feeling a feeling or being in an ego state that is undesirable at the moment. These awarenesses are part of the thinking process, and when you think, you automatically activate your Adult—the Adult becomes the executive or quarterback of your personality. It takes charge and either handles the situation itself or observes while the Nurturing Parent or Natural Child does so.

The easiest way to switch ego states is to talk to yourself out loud, when you are alone. When you actually hear your own thoughts spoken, any distortions in your thinking become much more apparent to you. This process also makes the Nurturing Parent, Adult, and Natural Child much more powerful and much more real to you. When it is not practical to talk to yourself out loud, a dialogue within your head will suffice—or, you can write down your thoughts and look at them. When you can see or hear your thoughts as if they came from someone else, this helps to clarify your thinking and helps you to distinguish between what you are thinking and what you are feeling. This process is one of the ways in which you can decontaminate your Adult, so that Parent and/or Child messages do not remain confused with Adult information and problem-solving ability.

A person can switch into Adult by thinking about almost anything. For example, while I wait in the dentist's chair for that humongous horse-needle my Child is scared of, I ask myself mathematical questions. Answering them keeps me in my Adult, so that I have less opportunity to experience my Child's fear. I believe that pain exists in the Child, and when I think (which is a function of my Adult) I do not feel the pain to the same degree. When I'm having an internal transaction, I may evaluate the Parent comments, or even the Child feelings, from an Adult, logical point of view to determine whether

32

they are sound. Another method I have found helpful is to trace back to when I first felt the feeling, how I started it, what I did or didn't do, and what I need to do now to be done with whatever undesirable feeling I am experiencing. When I get into my Adapted Child and feel inadequate, I find it very helpful to sort of step out of myself and say, "There is a little kid inside me who is feeling unsure. He needs some support from the grownup inside me." I then give myself a pep talk, or talk to my Child about his feelings in an understanding way. If I feel scared, I tell my Child that it is all right to feel scared and that I can be scared and still be effective at the same time. I might even decide to nurture myself in a physical way, like taking a hot shower. (Or, if I've just been rejected by a woman, a cold shower.) I might decide to make myself the kind of warm drink I found comforting when I was a child, or to have one of my favorite foods for dinner. There are any number of ways that I can help my Child feel better and then go on to do whatever it is I need to do.

With a little practice, you can learn to identify ego states easily— your own and other people's—and to stimulate the kinds of transactions that will fill your needs and get things done effectively.

Chapter III

WHY DO PEOPLE NEED STROKES?

It would be difficult to overemphasize the importance of strokes in our lives. Every human being has an innate *need* for stimuli from other human beings. We all need strokes whether or not we recognize this need: most emotional problems boil down to a lack of positive strokes.

Some years ago, a famous study by Dr. Rene Spitz[11] clearly indicated that infants require *physical* strokes for survival: unless babies are touched, they will die. As we grow older, our need for physical touching diminishes, though it never disappears. We learn to survive on non-physical strokes, to substitute any kind of attention for the physical strokes we still want and need. Negative attention will do if we cannot get positive attention. In other words, whether I hit you in the mouth, say that I hate you, give you a kiss, tell you that I like you, or look at you, I am giving you strokes that are needed by your Natural Child.

There are four kinds of strokes: *positive conditional, positive unconditional, negative conditional,* and *negative unconditional.* The word "conditional" means that I am stroking *behavior* ("You did a nice job on that," "I like the way you do your hair," etc.). "Unconditional" makes reference to stroking someone as a person (e.g., "I love you," "I hate you," not listening when somebody is talking to you, frowning at a person when he walks into the room). Conditional strokes are for *doing*; unconditional strokes are for *being.*

Examples of positive conditional strokes are: "You do good work," "I like your hair," "That's a beautiful sweater you're wearing," "You play a great game of tennis." Examples of unconditional positive strokes: a smile when you enter the room, a touch of friendship, asking your opinion on something, saying "I love you." A negative conditional stroke is when I tell you something I don't like about your behavior: "You did a poor job on that," "You're always making mistakes," "Your hair is too long," "Your table manners are atrocious." Examples of negative unconditional strokes are: name-calling, interrupting somebody in the middle of a sentence, failing to respond when spoken to, saying "I don't like you."

There is a place for positive conditional and positive unconditional strokes, since they lead to OK feelings for both the sender and the receiver and they take care of the Child need for strokes. There is also a place for *constructive* negative conditional strokes: we can learn from them, and we can use them to help others change their ineffective behavior patterns. Constructive negative conditional strokes come from Nurturing Parent, Adult, or Natural Child. For example, in response to your being late for our appointment, I can say from my Natural Child, "I'm angry at you for being late." I can say from my Adult, "Are you aware that you are 45 minutes late? Will you be on time next time?" I can say from my Nurturing Parent, "Please be on time." Because these negative strokes are *conditional* (I'm talking about your behavior, not about you as a person) and are from one of my effective ego states, it is easier for you to accept them.

Destructive negative conditional strokes tend to come from the Critical Parent or the Rebellious Child. In response to the same situation, the Critical Parent might say, "Don't you ever do what you say you're going to do? You're *never* on time!" The Rebellious Child might say, "I'm never waiting for you again! I'm always on time, and you're always late!" This is harder to accept, because it comes from one of my ineffective ego states. In fact, it may become a negative *un*conditional stroke if my tone of voice and facial expression indicate that you, as a person, are not OK. Clearly, if my aim is to help you change your behavior, I will want to make sure that my negative strokes are conditional and that they come from Nurturing Parent, Adult, or Natural Child.

There is no place for negative unconditional strokes, since their message is: "You are not-OK/bad/unimportant/worthless." Negative unconditional strokes are extremely destructive and have no redeeming social value whatsoever, yet many people invite such strokes and many are willing to administer them. When I become aware of the importance of strokes, I will seek positive strokes for myself, will give positive or constructive negative strokes, and will neither give nor accept negative unconditional strokes.

Why do people invite and accept negative strokes?

Remember, a stroke is a stroke. In terms of our survival needs, it doesn't really matter whether a stroke is negative or positive—every stroke counts toward the total, and *any* stroke is better than no stroke at all. People can get their stroking needs met from negative strokes, positive strokes, or any combination thereof. If I have not learned how to get enough positive strokes, I will invite negative strokes. If I don't get enough strokes for doing things right, I'll tend to do things wrong and get strokes for that.

Most of us are still operating on decisions we made about strokes when we were children. Each of us became accustomed to a certain level of stroking, to a certain mix of positive and negative strokes. We can change our decisions and give up our desire for negative strokes. Also, we can stop limiting the number of positive strokes we receive. In general, if people will accept, give and ask for positive strokes, they will diminish their tendency to seek negative strokes. If, on the other hand, they are accustomed to receiving negative strokes and tend to discount the giving and accepting of positive strokes, they will continue to invite and accept negative strokes in order to fulfill their stroking needs.

There is usually a correlation between how people accept positive or negative strokes and the general stroking pattern in their early family relationships. If people were given many positive strokes as children, they will have a better chance of accepting the positive and rejecting the negative—and vice versa. They are not "stuck with" the stroke economy they experienced as children, however. For example, a child growing up in a home with a negative stroke economy may make a decision to treat others differently from the way he was treated by Mom and Dad. When he becomes a parent, he will then do much better at giving positive strokes to his children than his parents did with him, because he has *made a decision* to change the stroke economy.

Businesses and families may have a positive or a negative stroke economy. For example, men in business will stroke each other regularly, in a sarcastic way. In the same organizations it is very rare for supervisors to give positive strokes; they generally give negative ones.

Our culture has many unwritten rules and myths about stroking. One of the myths is that there are not enough positive strokes to go around. There does seem to be a stroke shortage, but it is produced artificially by rules about who may give strokes to whom, and under what circumstances. There seems to be a general fear that if you give out too many strokes, you will run out of them. (Of course you will never run out of positive strokes!) It's against the rules to say nice things about yourself, or to directly say something nice about someone else. It's okay to be sarcastic, or to put yourself down. The rules say that it is not OK to ask for positive strokes, and that it is not OK to refuse strokes that you don't want. This is true in families and in businesses, as well as in social relationships. People who follow these rules often feel pretty helpless, since they think they have to take what they get and think they can't be straight about asking for what they want. If you're not straight about expressing your needs and wants, then you'll do it in a crooked fashion, outside of your Adult awareness. In all probability, you'll end up with negative rather than positive strokes if you follow the unwritten stroking rules.

When people discount their Natural Child need for strokes, getting what they want, or expressing their feelings, they will frequently eat, drink, smoke, purchase, play games, withdraw, get depressed, get sick, and so on. In essence, they are using crooked, indirect methods, which often don't work, to get what they want or to express how they feel. These old methods were learned in childhood when Natural Child needs and wants were not met. If you wonder whether you may be discounting your Natural Child, I invite you to make a mental or written note every time you reach for a cigarette, head for the refrigerator, or pour another drink. Just ask yourself, "What am I wanting, or feeling, that I am not expressing?" More often than not, you'll find that some want or feeling is being discounted. If you will go after what you want, or express how you feel, instead of engaging in any of the above behaviors, you will meet your needs and wants and get your feelings expressed much more satisfactorily. People who eat instead of getting strokes, expressing feelings, or filling some other want or need, often have severe weight problems. When I was teaching TA theory to a well-known weight-loss organization, they rapidly agreed with this point. I am convinced that weight loss is often only temporary because people have not developed a new method for expressing feelings and getting what they want. Consequently, they return to the old behavior and gain the weight back.

The stroking rules are even more strict and complex when *physical* strokes are involved. No doubt you can think of dozens of rules about who is allowed to touch whom, and when, and where, and how, and why. The result of these rules is that few people get as much physical stroking as they would like to have, and so most substitute other kinds of stroking but still feel as if something is missing from their lives. They may stroke themselves by eating too much, or drinking, or smoking. Many people buy things in order to stroke themselves or others. They give material things to others instead of the strokes they would like to give. We live in a society where eating, drinking, smoking and purchasing are OK and few "don'ts" are involved with them, so many of us try to fill our needs in those areas instead of in the more satisfying areas where there are far more prohibitions.

Why do people reject positive strokes?

As absurd as this may sound, in our culture it's "not polite" to simply *accept* positive strokes; most people have been taught to reject them in one way or another. For example, if someone compliments them they often fail to respond to the compliment at all (sometimes by quickly changing the subject) or actually deny it: "Oh, I really didn't do that job as well as I could have...." This kind of response is supposed to be polite, modest, and almost patriotic!

Often, instead of letting a stroke "sink in," people immediately start thinking of some response that will "pay the other person back." This sort of response dilutes the stroke so that it is less satisfying for both parties. It is sad but true that the majority of people manage to avoid receiving many positive strokes through dilution, denial, or diversion, even though they want and need those strokes.

On the other hand, most people have been taught that they *must accept* negative strokes. It's usually easy to tell when people are accepting negative strokes—they look angry, hurt, defensive, etc.— and to see that such strokes are getting through to them with a lot of impact. Most of these negative strokes are not constructive, and are neither needed nor wanted by the recipients, so why take them in? Steiner suggests that it makes much better sense to accept positive strokes and to reject negative ones. I certainly agree—it makes much more sense to charge my battery positively than it does to charge it negatively. Clearly we do have a way of filtering strokes; otherwise, we would not be successful in keeping out the positive ones and allowing the negative ones to enter with full force. With practice, we can learn to overcome the old stroking rules, reverse this screening process, and permit the entry of positive strokes while allowing destructive negative strokes to bounce off. We can also utilize negative strokes that do contain helpful information for us: we can let in and use the information but keep out any invitations to feel bad that might be sent along with it. By screening them in this way, we can learn from these negative strokes without feeling angry, hurt or defensive, and we avoid missing information or feedback about our behavior that can be helpful to us. Healthy, OK people do not-OK things from time to time. They are willing to accept criticism, filter it, and use it for their growth.

How can I accept positive strokes and get others to accept them from me?

If you receive a positive stroke, give it a second to "sink in" and then simply say "Thank you!" If you do feel the stroke, you'll proba- bly smile. Notice how a youngster accepts a positive stroke: there is usually a big, spontaneous grin and a look of delight. This is also true with adults—a smile and a "thank you" are usually clear indications of the acceptance of a stroke. If you give a person a compliment and he or she uses a maneuver to reject it, simply ask the person to accept the compliment. This can be done in a light way, from Child: "Boy, I just gave you a compliment and you didn't accept it!" Or, "Please take my compliment."

You can also reject negative strokes with a light touch. I was singing to a woman recently, and she responded to this by asking me, "What did you do with the money?" I asked, "What money?" She replied, "The money your mother gave you for singing lessons." Instead of feeling bad, I grinned and commented, "I thought you had a better ear for music than that."

How can I get more positive strokes?

There are four ways of getting strokes: performing, asking for them, giving them to others, and giving them to yourself. When you "perform," you do something designed to elicit some sort of praise or compliment. Performing will often get you a positive, conditional stroke. For example, I like to teach TA because I am doing a service and additionally, I very much enjoy the strokes I get for doing a good job of teaching. It seems to me that most people get the majority of their positive strokes by performing. Sometimes people carry this to extremes, however. They do things just to get strokes, rather than because they enjoy doing them, and end up spending a lot of time doing things that they don't really enjoy.

When you're wanting a stroke and not getting it, I invite you to ask for it. Make this as specific as possible; e. g. (employee to boss) "How do you think I did on that budget report?" or "In what ways do you think I'm doing a good job?" When I invite people to ask for strokes in this way, there is usually a barrage of "Yes, but..." and

"I'd never do that," and "They'll give you a stroke, all right, but they won't really mean it," and "What good is it if you have to ask for it?" To begin with, if I'm wanting something and I'm not getting it, by asking for it I either break even or win. If my request is rejected (and notice I said *my request,* not *me,* because I retain the exclusive right to define my OK-ness as a person), I haven't lost anything. Asking for strokes is often difficult because people are afraid that they will be rejected. It is important to remember that rejection of a request is NOT a rejection of YOU. If you ask from an "I'm OK" position and the other person does not choose to respond in the way you would like, you are still OK. You are still breaking even. It's more likely, however, that a request from the "I'm OK" position will elicit the response you want; the odds are pretty good that you'll win if you are willing to ask for positive strokes. In sales organizations, this is perhaps the biggest problem that salespeople have: they tend to be afraid that, if they ask for the sale, they will be rejected personally. In reality, the other person is rejecting only the request or the proposition. They cannot reject you.

There is some basis for the widespread fear that asked-for strokes will be insincere. This probably stems from the fact that *many* strokes "don't feel right" and may be hard to accept because they are coming from the other person's Adapted Child. Some people give strokes, not because they "want to" from Natural Child or Nurturing Parent, but because they "should" give them. They are under orders, from their Parent or somebody else's, and their Adapted Child is complying with these orders. It is no wonder that such strokes come across in an insincere way. For example, some people are careful to give gifts that cost roughly the same amount as the gifts that were given to them, or they give away gifts because of the time of year and not because there is any real desire to give to someone else. At those times when my Natural Child was not invested in giving, what I gave and how it was received were diminished. I used to buy gifts based solely upon what I thought someone else would like, whether or not I liked the gift myself. I found that if I checked to see whether I really wanted to give a gift, and asked myself in greater depth what I wanted to give, the result was that the recipient and I both enjoyed the gift much more. If you are worried about eliciting an insincere response from someone, you can make a request for strokes that begins like this: "I really would like to know where you stand. Will you please give me honest feedback on the question I am about to ask you?" Then make the request.

Sometimes positive strokes don't "feel right" simply because you are not used to receiving them or are still listening to Parent messages that say "Don't accept positive strokes—it's not polite," or "you don't deserve them," or "you shouldn't take strokes for that because it isn't perfect," and so on. I invite you to practice receiving and enjoying positive strokes.

Another reason that some strokes don't "feel right" is that they are what Claude Steiner[12] calls "Plastic Fuzzies." They might look good on the surface, but they contain something negative that we don't want to accept. A Plastic Fuzzy is rather like a sugar-coated pill. We may swallow it and then notice that we are left with a bad taste. If I said to a woman, "Wow, you really think like a man," that's likely to be a Plastic Fuzzy for her. It contains an implied criticism ("Women don't think as well as men; you're a woman; too bad, but you're doing really well anyway, dear!") that she may not want to accept. If so, she can "clean up" the stroke. She can take the part she likes ("Wow, you really think effectively!") and refuse to take the part she doesn't want. You do not have to take any stroke you don't want, even if it's a positive stroke. You can choose to take only the strokes you like, the strokes that are good for you. If you are presented with a Plastic Fuzzy and you like part of it, you can take that part and throw the rest away.

A good reason to ask for strokes is that doing so can help loosen up a tight stroke economy; that is, it's another way of getting more strokes in circulation. If you model for others that it is OK to ask for and accept positive strokes, this can be contagious. It's likely that your associates will begin to ask for, receive, and accept more positive strokes as a result of your modeling. If you give strokes freely, this gives people permission to give strokes to you. (For example, I've often complimented women I date for their excellent taste in men.) Again, permission is given by modeling the kind of behavior that you expect. If you are giving strokes simply because you want to, others will usually respond by doing the same.

As I have said before, giving strokes is one way of getting strokes. I am not suggesting, however, that you give strokes exclusively for purposes of getting strokes in return. People often sense this intuitively and do not respond in kind. Strokes given only to get some in return are really Plastic Fuzzies and not sincere. If you stroke people because you genuinely want to, however, the result is that you are often on the receiving end of appropriate strokes from them. When you give people strokes, you are modeling that it is OK for them to give strokes to you. Modeling is the most powerful type of permission. I have noted that when parents or top management in a company are willing to openly give strokes to people, an atmosphere is created in which they also receive positive strokes from those around them. People often have positive things to say about others and can easily find sincere comments to make which would genuinely be appreciated.

The fourth way of getting strokes is to stroke yourself, in your head and out loud as well. I often find that when I say something nice about myself out loud, people begin to laugh, and others smirk. I am violating the stroking rules, and that's almost un-American! I am comforted by what a famous rabbi, Hillel, said several hundred years ago: "If I am not for myself, who will be for me? If I am only for myself, what am I? And, if not now, when?" I *know* it is OK to stroke myself. The nervous laughter I sometimes hear from people who are just learning about TA stems from their recognition that it just MIGHT be OK to break those old rules and start getting the strokes they want and need. Their Child ego states might be getting a kick out of seeing somebody break the rules. Again, I am modeling new behaviors for others, behaviors that I am convinced will work well for them.

When I say nice things about myself, it is not necessary to put anyone else down. Doing so produces a common form of "bragging" that is really objectionable; for example, "When *I* teach transactional analysis, I do it the *right* way." Please notice the implied "They're-Not-OK" message in that. However, when I stroke myself in a sincere and accurate way (e.g., "When I teach transactional analysis, I really do a good job"), this is not objectionable except to the Critical Parent of certain people. I think it's worth mentioning again that many people spend their lives in a futile attempt to adapt to other peoples' Critical Parents: "What will *they* think?" The Critical Parent in my head, and other peoples' Critical Parents, by definition will not EVER accept me, so I have chosen not to be concerned about the prejudicial part of other people or myself. If I'm invested in a relationship with someone, I do want that person to like me from Natural Child, to think I'm bright from Adult, and to be empathetic from Nurturing Parent. I have no concern about getting acceptance from a part of that person which will never accept me. This does not mean that I would not accept constructive criticism about my behavior from that person's Critical Parent; I would, however, use my own filtration system to determine whether the criticism is sound. In essence, I would "strain out" the Critical Parent component and admit only the factual, Adult information contained in the criticism. I owe it to myself to objectively hear and respond to any kinds of comments that will be helpful to me, regardless of source.

As I mentioned before, I can also stroke myself in my head. My Nurturing Parent can give supportive, complimentary and comforting strokes to my Natural Child at any time, especially at those times when my Child can really use a stroke. If I'm feeling bad, I can say to myself, "There is a little kid inside you that is feeling some pain, or is really stroke-hungry, so give him what he needs." I can remember that my Nurturing Parent was developed to take care of ME, in the beginning, and is still needed for that purpose. One of the richest sources of stroking for me has been my own Nurturing Parent. I remember an occasion when I had decided to confront a very well known transactional analyst in front of a thousand people. My little Kid was scared and needed reassurance, so I said, from Nurturing Parent, things like, "You'll do a good job. You really understand people well." With this and other reassuring messages, my frightened Child felt better and I was effective with my confrontation.

I urge you to use your Adult to examine the stroking rules and decide which ones you wish to keep and which you wish to disregard. You will probably be surprised to see how much more often it is OK to stroke and be stroked, to touch and be touched. Why not hug your son, or your best friend? Why not give someone an unconditional stroke if you feel like it? Why not say nice things about yourself, out loud? If you use your Adult to guide your behavior, and stop following harmful rules about stroking, you can multiply the positive strokes you give and receive. If you have difficulty asking for, or accepting, or giving, positive strokes, you can practice any one of these behaviors. Although it may feel awkward at first, and you may feel like it's "not you," the behavior will soon become second nature. The results of giving, accepting, and asking for strokes are very positive. By doing these things, you will invite others to do the same.

Chapter IV

WHY DO PEOPLE KEEP DOING THE SAME THINGS OVER AND OVER AGAIN?

We have all seen people who "almost" make it, or who fail again and again, or who don't really start living until some particular event takes place (e.g., "When the kids are through with college we'll begin to enjoy some time away"), or who seem bent on self-destruction. They are following the life scripts that they developed as children. Though they may have little or no conscious awareness of these life plans, nevertheless they are clearly carrying them out.

What is a life script?

A script is an unsatisfactory life plan developed in early childhood, under parental influence, which directs the individual's behavior in the most important aspects of his life. Often the plots of people's life scripts can be found in specific fairytales or stories. Like fairytales, scripts can have happy, tragic, or uninteresting courses and consequences. I see scripts as *unsatisfactory* life plans, even if they have "happy" endings, because they are the result of decisions made on the basis of incomplete (and often erroneous) information. These decisions are made from Adapted Child, in conjunction with a clever Little Professor that unfortunately is relatively uninformed; therefore, script decisions that had survival value in childhood are usually useless or harmful in adult life. Here's an example of a script decision that may have been beneficial in childhood: If I got hit for showing anger as a child and therefore decided not to show anger, that was clearly a sound decision at the time. As an adult, however, it is harmful for me to keep my anger in, and it is no longer dangerous for me to express this feeling, so it is important for me to change that decision I made when I was little. The major goal in transactional analysis is to identify script decisions and, from Adult and Natural Child, to change these decisions so that behavior can be autonomous rather than "script-driven."

There are two categories of destructive Parent messages: "don't" messages, called *injunctions,* and "do" messages, called *directives.* Often the directives either support the injunctions or contradict them; directives are often referred to as *counter-injunctions.* Children decide whether to comply with, rebel against, or essentially ignore the injunctions and directives, and these are the script decisions that form the basis for their life plans. Youngsters often identify with a person in a mythical or real story, which they use as a model for how to follow the script decisions.

After the script story or plot is chosen, the next step is to select a cast of characters who will fit into the general plot. For example, if I have made a script decision not to get close to a woman, then I will tend to select women who don't want to get close. I do this intuitively, with my Little Professor, and again may have little or no conscious awareness of what I am doing. I may believe that I am looking for a woman who wants to get close—and she probably believes the same—yet we have each found someone who will help us to advance our scripts. Another way I could carry out a script decision not to get close would be to choose people who are unavailable. For example, at one time I was attracted to women who lived out of town, or who were "hard to get." Obviously, the chances of getting close to such women were limited.

I play psychological games with my cast of characters in order to support whatever script decisions I've made. These games end in bad feelings and deteriorated relationships that are all part of my life plan. (Games will be covered in more detail in Chapter V.) I use my cast of characters to help me collect my favorite kinds of bad feelings. Script-supporting feelings, when collected, are called *stamps*. These "feelings stamps" are like the trading stamps that could be collected and turned in for premiums. Once I have several books full of stamps, I can cash them in for the right to do something I decided to do a long time ago (get a divorce, be alone, fly into a rage, etc.). With a big enough collection, I can cash in my stamps for a "free" nervous breakdown, suicide, or murder.

How will learning about scripts help me as a manager or supervisor?

People tend to act out their scripts within organizations as well as within their families. They select the kind of organization and the kind of supervisor or boss that will permit them to stay in their scripts. For example, if a person feels like a loser and believes he will never be accepted, it's likely that he will select the kind of organization or supervisor who will not accept him. He will take a job that is likely to "prove" that he is a loser. Also, personnel directors tend to select employees on the basis of their own script beliefs and decisions. This is exemplified by the male personnel director who believes that women are childlike and who therefore is willing to consider hiring women only for subordinate positions. When individuals select characters to help advance their scripts, this usually also helps advance the scripts of the people selected.

Scripts are generated within families. Organizations have many of the same elements that can be found in a typical family. Within organizations, and even within individual departments, there are parent figures who send both positive and destructive messages, and there are the "children" who blindly accept the messages, or rebel against them. The subordinates often make decisions that are not to their benefit, and then live them out within the organizational structure. Elements such as sibling rivalry, game-playing and stamp collecting exist within organizations, just as they do within families. It can even be said that organizations themselves have scripts. Parent messages frequently originate from the founding fathers of the organization and are passed on, generation after generation, from department to department. As we discuss the common types of destructive Parent messages, we will see how these messages also exist within organizations.

What are the most common injunctions?

Here are eleven of the basic destructive injunctions,[13] along with behavior that often results from accepting them. My experience indicates that the average person has received three to five of these injunctions and has followed two or three of them.

The first of these injunctions is simply *"Don't."* This injunction is sent to a youngster by continual "don't" responses that make it appear that very little of his behavior is OK. If the youngster decides to follow this injunction, he will end up manifesting a great deal of Compliant Child behavior; he will be afraid to make decisions, to be assertive, etc.

Employees are often given repetitive "don't" messages and, as a result, feel that little of their work is acceptable. They sort of toss in the towel and agree blindly to do things they are told to do, even though those things may not make sense. These employees are afraid to be assertive, to be creative, and to express their own thoughts.

The *"Don't Be"* injunction is a result of rejection, both verbal and non-verbal. Often physical abuse is a key element. If the youngster decides to follow this injunction, he will end up manifesting behavior

47

which can kill him, slowly or rapidly; e.g., excessive drinking, eating or smoking, reckless driving, engaging in dangerous work or leisure activities, picking the "wrong" people to confront or fight with. Another manifestation of a decision to follow the "Don't Be" is a further decision not to enjoy life: "Maybe it's OK if I survive, if I don't really live." The Little Professor hits on a decision to not enjoy life as a way of placating the parent who he believes is telling him not to be, and at the same time taking care of his Natural Child desire to live. Some people who are following this injunction seem afraid to admit, even to themselves, that there is anything good about their lives. They manage to be unhappy and unsatisfied, no matter what, and have difficulty in recognizing any positive feelings in themselves. If things go too well, they're likely to feel nervous and apprehensive until they can manage to make things go wrong again. Part of them believes that any enjoyment of life is a real threat to survival, but they generally do not have conscious awareness of this belief and its origins. They continue to live flat, joyless lives: "It's OK if I live, as long as I don't enjoy it." Some people justify their right to live by following parental directives to "Be Perfect," work very hard, please people, etc., so that their parent won't resent having them. Because they are following these directives as a matter of survival, it is very difficult for them to stop doing so until *after* they have decided not to follow the "Don't Be" injunction. For example, say that an individual is a "workaholic" in order to justify his right to live. If his therapist helps him to work less (without first addressing the problem of the "Don't Be"), the individual may become very depressed and even suicidal. If you are following a "Don't Be" injunction, it is very important to clear that up first. Your other redecisions will then be much easier.

The *"Don't Be You"* injunction often means that you're not supposed to be the sex that you are. For example, a male may be given a female name and encouraged to take on what used to be a stereotypical female role; i.e., he is encouraged to do housework, take care of others, be passive and quiet rather than a roughneck, et cetera. Later on, he is often told that Daddy or Mommy really wanted a little girl rather than a little boy. According to the Gouldings, in single-sex families the oldest girl may become Daddy's little boy and the youngest boy may become Mommy's little girl. Youngsters who decide to follow this injunction may end up with some sexual difficulty—fear of sex, homosexuality, impotence, etc. This injunction also covers the issue of whether I am going to be what *I* want to be, or what you want me to be. If a child decides to follow the "Don't Be You" injunction, she may adopt a role that someone else wants her to play, or may live someone else's life. She may be "Daddy's little angel" or an extension of Mommy whose job it is to do what Mommy wanted to do and couldn't. William Smith, Jr., often is supposed to be like his father. People who have bought "Don't Be You" tend to have the vague feeling that something is wrong, that *they* are in the wrong—in the wrong body, the wrong profession, the wrong relationship. They may be in doubt about who they are and what they really want, may be constantly trying to change themselves in some way, may go from guru to guru and from group to group, looking for someone or something that will give them a sense of identity and integration. They manifest Compliant Child and Rebellious Child behavior, either trying to be like someone else or trying *not* to be like someone else. They're often out of touch with (or suspicious of) the needs, wants and feelings of their Natural Child. Following the "Don't Be You" injunction makes it hard to know, accept and love oneself, and without self-love, it is difficult to love others. Accepting this injunction can therefore promote a frustrating existence.

Within organizations, it is common for people to be invited to do the job the way it has always been done, or to do the job the way their predecessor did it. They are discouraged or prevented from using their own initiative and from changing the old, established ways. In essence, they are told "Don't Be You," do the job the way it has always been done. People who accept this injunction tend to lack initiative and usually fail to push for necessary changes.

The injunction of *"Don't Be a Child"* is often given to the oldest child in the family, when one or both parents are eager for her to grow up and help take care of the other children. This youngster is encouraged to take on adult-like responsibilities and is discouraged from playing, having fun, and being a little kid. People who decide to follow this injunction have great difficulty playing, having fun, taking vacations, and enjoying life in general. They tend not to use their Child ego states.

All too frequently, people are told that when they are on the job they are not to play, have fun, and really enjoy it. They are supposed to be serious and not "waste time" in talking to their fellow employees, in socializing together, because such behavior is seen as a detriment to getting the job done. In my opinion, the opportunity to get one's Natural Child stroked within an organization provides the energy needed for people to get the job done effectively. Unfortunately, the "Don't Be a Child" message predominates in many organizations, and circulation of energy-giving strokes is severely impaired.

The *"Don't Grow Up"* injunction is often given to the youngest child in the family when the parents' relationship is less than satisfying. Again without Adult awareness, one or both parents infantilize the youngster; that is, they do many more things for him than he needs done, so as to have him stay dependent and therefore, they hope, never leave them alone with one another by going away to school, etc. The "Don't Grow Up" will often manifest itself in school phobias and in a real crisis at age 18 when it's time to go away to school. A typical result is the "Mama's boy" who at age 45 is still living at home, on the one hand dependent upon Mama and on the other hand taking care of Mama.

Many people are invited not to grow up within organizations. They are infantilized, given very precise, structured directions for doing their jobs, and are not invited to make decisions and assume responsibility. Often a supervisor is fearful that, if people grow up and become independent within the structure, he will be vulnerable and may lose his job. The truth is that when a supervisor helps people to be as independent as is necessary and advisable to complete their work effectively, that supervisor's effectiveness and potency has increased tremendously.

"Don't Get Close" is an injunction transmitted by parents' avoidance of intimacy. They do not desire to get emotionally or physically close to the youngster and often will not get close to one another. The youngster will then manifest great difficulty in establishing close relationships with other people and in sharing intimate feelings and ideas.

Within organizational structures, all too frequently, people are invited not to get close. One predominant idea is that supervisors are not to share anything of their personal lives or the feelings and thoughts they have inside them, for fear that doing so would make them vulnerable and diminish their effectiveness. Supervisors are therefore invited to "Be Strong" and keep things to themselves. This fallacious idea keeps people at a distance and provides a sterile atmosphere in which people's investment in their work, in the company, and in their co-workers is minimal. Ultimately, the bottom line suffers. Of course, it is vital for people to use their Adults for determining what kinds of information to reveal, to whom, and under what circumstances. Healthy people have a filtration system which permits them to be appropriately close.

"Don't Feel" injunctions are a result of negative responses to any displays of Natural Child emotions such as mad, sad, glad or scared. In some families, however, the "Don't Feel" is more specific in that it is OK to feel certain feelings but not OK to feel other feelings that are not approved of in the family. The youngster who decides to follow this injunction has difficulty with the healthy expression of any or all of the four basic feelings. The "Don't Feel" injunction is more often given to little boys concerning feelings of fear, sadness, and tenderness, while little girls are not supposed to feel anger or sexual feelings. Boys will tend to express the "acceptable" feeling of anger when they're scared, while girls will feel hurt and cry when they are really angry.

"Don't Feel" is perhaps the most common injunction that I see within organizations. For some reason, thinking is at a premium and seems to be the only mental process that is acceptable. Many supervisors model being the Rock of Gibralter and have a misguided concept of strength. They believe that when they are "strong" (that is, when they don't show their mads, sads, scareds, uncertainty) they will be seen as potent and will be followed and respected. I believe that when they express these human qualities to the people around them, their potency increases tremendously. Discounting of feelings leads to ineffectiveness within the organization.

The *"Don't Think"* message is given to children, and especially to little girls, when they are not encouraged to share their ideas and to figure things out for themselves. Such children are not expected to be reasonable, rational, or informed: they're not expected to develop their Adult ego states. Youngsters who follow this injunction are often confused and, when a situation calls for thinking, tend to emote rather than figure things out. According to Steiner, alcoholics often have decided to follow a "Don't Think" injunction and drink in order *not* to think.[14]

The "Don't Think" message predominates in many organizations when the key leaders trust only themselves and their own thinking abilities. They are unwilling to delegate responsibility and to invite their subordinates to use their own minds in the resolution of problems and the making of decisions. I still find it rather rare to encounter females in top management positions. Historically, of course, women were not supposed to think and were not seen as capable of making major decisions and assuming major responsibilities. Organizations that invite employees to think are the organizations that prosper.

"Don't Succeed" is a common injunction that is transmitted by stroking the child for failing as well as by not allowing the youngster to experience success. For example, a child who is trying to master a simple task will not experience success if he is stopped or "helped" in the middle of the job. He will be laughed at when he stumbles and falls, or he will be given negative strokes for doing poorly. The "Don't Succeed" person often exhibits such behaviors as getting close to success and then failing, or actually doing something well but nevertheless feeling that it's not good enough and that he "should have done it better." "Don't Succeed" is not necessarily a directive to fail; some who follow this injunction simply engage in a no-win, no-lose manner and "just get by" in life. Although they haven't clearly failed at anything, their lives are not very satisfying to them, either. The directive to "Be Perfect" often goes along with a "Don't Succeed" injunction. This directive invites failure and frustration because it is almost impossible to succeed at "Being Perfect."

In the typical structure of supervision, the supervisor strokes people mostly for the errors they make. Errors get attention; that is, when a mistake or failure occurs, this seems to be an acceptable time to talk to a subordinate. The subordinate is not talked to when she succeeds or when things are simply progressing smoothly. It appears that the moral of this story is, if you want attention from your boss, don't succeed. Also, I have seen many examples of how subordinates are invited to fail by being given tasks that they don't want, or don't have the ability to carry out, and then are not supported effectively in assuming those responsibilities.

The *"Don't Have Needs of Your Own"* injunction is often modeled by a parent who is "living for" her child: she overworks, is self-sacrificing, and will rarely say what she wants. In essence, she is modeling how to be a Rescuer and end up a Victim. The youngster is often thwarted in his desires, if not overtly scolded for "wanting." In following this injunction, people are often Rescuers and, like most Rescuers, end up as Victims. Their apparent nurturing is done from Compliant Child because they "should" nurture. They tend to be out of touch with their needs and not know what they want. If they do happen to know what they need or want, rarely will they ask for it

52

directly. They generally feel guilty for having needs or wants and often see themselves as "selfish."

All too frequently, organizations neglect to tune in to the needs and wants of their employees. The focus is on the needs of the organization, and the legitimate desires and complaints of the people within the organization are discounted. The Natural Child needs of the employee for a decent place to work, to eat, to rest, are often neglected. Likewise, reasonable salaries, fringe benefits, vacations, and sick leave have been neglected. Many individuals whose needs have been discounted by the companies who employ them have chosen collective bargaining as a way of ameliorating the problem. Organizations that have been willing to take into account the needs of their employees—with reasonable benefits, salaries, and working hours as well as with positive recognition—have happier, more creative, more committed employees. Again, the bottom line benefits.

"Don't Be Sane" is a rather lethal injunction that is sent to youngsters through stroking of their erratic or bizarre behavior. In general, a "Don't Be Sane" message is promoted when a youngster has to act in extreme ways in order to get attention. I am reminded of a youngster who used to put on his helmet and run into the wall, behavior that was stroked by his parents' laughter. A "Don't Be Sane" message is often reinforced by parental modeling of bizarre behavior as well as by tolerance of and encouragement of the child's own extreme behavior. The family's tolerance of "crazy" behavior in its members often leads the child to believe that he'll end up crazy just like Mama, Auntie, or Grandpa; he may have some fantasy that it's hereditary. People who have made a "Don't Be Sane" decision often manifest extremely neurotic or psychotic behaviors.

Approximately two out of three injunctions are sent by the parent of the opposite sex, while the parent of the same sex models the behavior. For example, Mom frowns at the boy for crying; Daddy shows the boy how to conceal sad feelings through being a stoic himself. Of course, this makes sense, since Mom, who has made a decision that men shouldn't show feelings, has chosen to marry a man who doesn't show feelings.

How do these injunctions appear in a person's script?

To illustrate, I've invented some case histories that are composites of people I've read about, seen, or heard about from others. The first patient is a young man of 18 who was referred to a psychiatrist because of suicidal threats. This young man's social history revealed that he had been born to parents who were in their late forties. He had been told, by the way he was treated and responded to from early childhood on, that he really wasn't wanted (a "Don't Be" injunction). His parents spent little time with him, and on several occasions they were physically abusive. Later on, when he could understand verbal messages, he was told that he was "an accident," not wanted, and that ever since he was born he had been "nothing but trouble." (This last, by the way, can amount to a directive to *continue* to make trouble.) At some time during his grade-school years he decided that he would eventually kill himself, because he believed that was what his parents really wanted (Script Decision); he decided to comply with their wishes. (Sometimes people decide to kill themselves from a rebellious position in which they might think something like "I'll kill myself, and I'll show *them*! Then I'll be around to see how unhappy they are!") I say that he made this decision in grade school because his case history showed that he made a bona fide suicide attempt when he was in the sixth grade. Throughout his teenage years he remained virtually friendless and alone, predominantly because of the way he dealt with people. For example, he would agree to meet someone at a certain time, and then not show up. Or, he would say the wrong thing at the wrong time to the wrong person and then get beaten up or rejected in other ways (the game of Kick Me). He would then end up feeling depressed, lonely, and hurt. He built up these bad feelings (collected stamps) over a period of several years and then made another bona fide suicide attempt (tried to cash in his collection).

In another case, a young woman in crisis sought the assistance of a psychiatric social worker. The problem she presented was that she had just received a bill for a large amount of money she spent in a local department store. As she related the story, she indicated that she was very upset with herself because "this is just another way I'm driving my husband away." When asked how that worked, she said, "When I spend a lot of money, my husband gets very angry at me and threatens to leave me" (a game). She was asked why she wanted to drive her husband away. She replied that she wasn't sure but thought it might have something to do with a decision she made at the age of 12, following her father's sudden death. She had loved and trusted her father, and he left her. She therefore decided never to trust men again (Script Decision). As the interview progressed she indicated that, as a teenager and young adult in the dating world, when a man was warm and friendly, for some unknown reason she didn't like him; however, if he were stand-offish, devious, said one thing and did another, for some unknown reason she gravitated toward him (Character Selection). Sure enough, they would date for a while, and she would run through a series of disappointments and rejections, one after another. The man would tell her that he wanted to get close, and then he would complain that they were getting *too* close. On the other hand, she would invite him to share feelings and then would withdraw from him when he did so (a psychological game called Rapo). Finally, she married a man who was not very giving, not very nurturing, and had a low tolerance for her behavior in general. She had a whole list of bad feelings pent up in her. At this point in the interview, it became clear that they were headed for divorce because she was ready to cash in her stamps for "one free divorce."

Many of us are involved in milder versions of similar scripts, as a result of decisions we made when we were very young.

Are you saying that I could be letting a five-year-old child direct my life?

Most people are carrying out a life script developed by a little child. This explains much of people's contrary, illogical, driving, violent, compulsive and self-destructive behavior: many people are driven by their scripts. A goal of transactional analysis is to change scripts and lead autonomous rather than script-driven lives.

Script decisions are made somewhere between the ages of three and sixteen. I emphasize that the decisions are MADE BY ME, for myself, and NOT by my parents. This emphasis is extremely important, because the realization that the decisions are my own gives me the power to change the decisions instead of doggedly living with them and blaming my parents for my lot in life. As mentioned earlier, script decisions are made by my Adapted Child in conjunction with my Little Professor. The decisions are my own and are reflections of my unique personality, which is one explanation for the fact that, within the same family, one child can be a hardened criminal and another a successful businessman. I'm reminded of the story of three boys who were caught at the scene of a sex crime. Since the authorities did not know which of the boys had committed the crime, they sent the youngsters to a psychologist for psychological testing.

One at a time, the first two boys properly identified a circle as a circle, a square as a square, and a triangle as a triangle. The third boy, however, identified the circle as a naked woman, the triangle as a naked woman, and the square as a naked woman. When confronted by the psychologist about his "sexual problems," the boy replied, *"Me?* You're the one who's showing those dirty pictures!" The third boy, when confronted with the same stimuli as the other two, came to quite a different decision about the meaning of the stimuli.

Jacqui Schiff makes the point that these script decisions, although initially made by the Adapted Child and the Little Professor, are later incorporated into the child's own Parent ego state. As a result of this incorporation, the person's internal Parent regularly re-states the decisions to the person's Child. This, by the way, is an example of Parent content contributed by the individual himself rather than by parent figures.

Decisions are often made for reasons of survival. Every little kid wants to be loved—or, if not loved, at least to be taken care of well enough to survive. Youngsters therefore will do almost anything to get taken care of, even if it means abiding by destructive messages. It is important to note that these decisions are often the soundest ones a child can make, given his circumstances: e.g., if my father beats me up when I show feelings, it's damn smart of me to quit showing feelings. The problem, however, is that I hold on to these early decisions, even in my adult life. Would you ask a five-year-old how to run your life? According to script theory, that same five- or six-year-old is still calling the shots.

My parents were great. Why would I make destructive script decisions?

It is important to note that, although TA focuses on the not-OK messages that parents send to their children, we are very cognizant of the fact that most parents also send many OK messages and do not mean to send the not-OK ones. The injunctions are sent *outside the Adult awareness* of the parents, from Mom and Dad's Adapted Child, and they are often the same injunctions that Mom and Dad received from their own parents. For example, a mother might not want her little boy to cry because she decided in childhood (based upon programming from her own parents) that little boys shouldn't cry. She loves her son and wouldn't dream of doing him harm, but if he begins to cry, she may frown, or scold him, or send him to his room, because of her belief that he "shouldn't" cry. The boy receives a message of "Don't Cry" which can be generalized to a "Don't Show Feelings" or "Don't Feel" injunction, a message she would not have sent him deliberately. In other words, the healthy ego states in Mom and Dad do not send destructive messages to their offspring. Most parents truly care about their children and do the best job of parenting they can, within the limitations of their own scripts. The problem is that injunctions are transmitted by the general, predominant attitude of one or both parents toward the child during his first 30 months of life, and these attitudes are often determined by not-OK messages that are passed down from generation to generation, some of which are outside the conscious awareness of the parents. Therefore, despite the loving care that we may have received as children, most of us have made destructive script decisions that interfere with our adult lives until we examine and change those decisions.

Simply by pushing away a child who wants to be next to Mama, a "don't bother me" message is sent. If the pushing-away happens frequently, perhaps because Mama is overworked or busy with the pressing demands of a new baby, the child may interpret it as a "Don't Exist" message. I hasten to say that very few parents really want their child to kill himself; the key issue, however, is the youngster's *perception* of the meaning of his parent's responses to him— and the decisions *he* makes as a result of those perceptions.

Why don't people just drop their scripts when they grow up?

People tend to hold on to their scripts because of the discomfort they may feel when they break injunctions (that is, when they change their script decisions). Even though they have plenty of Adult information to the effect that they don't need to follow those old injunctions anymore, their Parent ego states remain unconvinced. When people break injunctions, they often report that their Parent messages increase in strength and volume, or they feel guilty or scared, or they experience all these unpleasant sensations at once. The Compliant Child starts feeling the same fears or stresses that it experienced when making the original decision to follow that injunction. Because of this discomfort, people often return to the adapted behavior. For example, a woman who had a "Don't Have Needs of Your Own" injunction had decided that she would play golf for a change, instead of chauffeuring her teenage son to his weekly tennis game.

As she was driving to the course, she began to hear her Parent say, "What kind of mother are you? How could you do that to your boy?" She immediately felt so guilty that she turned around and drove back home. One reason that therapy is useful at the point of redecision is that it offers an external, "more powerful" Parent who can offer protection from the individual's internal Parent messages. When you break decisions, it is often helpful to switch ego states and comfort your scared Child, be logical, or ask your friends for understanding and support.

I don't like my script. How can I change it?

Scripts are the result of decisions, and anything that has been *decided* can be *redecided*. One of the primary reasons for knowing my own script is that I am then in a good position to make script redecisions. Since *I* made the decision originally, it's up to me to change it. Fortunately, I can change my decisions *at any age*. My next task will be to get some help in implementing the changes; e.g., if I decide to start showing my feelings, it becomes important for me to have some modeling or therapy for effective expression of feelings. One phenomenon I have recognized as a therapist is that when I first begin to show my feelings I will have a tendency to do so from Adapted Child and Critical Parent. Jon Weiss has said that this is like turning on a faucet that hasn't been used for a long time: what comes out at first may be polluted and filled with debris. After a while, however, the water begins to run clear. So don't worry if the first feelings to come up are not-OK feelings. Fine—you have started allowing your feelings to flow and, as in developing any skill, the most important thing is to *begin*. I won't ever learn to play tennis if I don't get out on the court and start playing. As I practice my swing, I will begin to hit the ball over the net more often than not. If I play daily, and have a pro to help me with my timing, etc., I will soon become able to return the ball even to expert players who know my weak spots. Eventually I'll become well coordinated and play automatically, without having to think about it. Behavior change through transactional analysis is a similar process.

There are many ways to make script redecisions. Many people have done so without help; that is, they have changed jobs, ended destructive relationships, changed ineffective behaviors and attitudes, without the external support of therapy. There is little doubt, however, that it is often more efficient—and an absolute necessity in some cases—to seek psychotherapeutic assistance. This is especially true when people have been "trying" to change destructive behaviors with little or no success. Please don't misunderstand: psychotherapy is *not* exclusively for psychoceramics (crackpots)! Even *I*, difficult as it may be to believe, was in psychotherapy for 18 months. It was a breath of fresh air and the best investment of my life.

TA has borrowed from the Gestaltists the concept of change in the here-and-now. If you will change your thinking and/or your feeling and/or your behavior (what you say or do), you are in essence changing your script decisions. For example, if I remember to say "I feel angry" instead of "You make me angry," it's likely that I will feel relieved instead of remaining angry. Simply by using my Adult to remember to change my words, I change my behavior, which results in changing my feelings. This sequence is counter to my "Don't Show Feelings" injunction. Each time I successfully break an injunction, it grows weaker.

A helpful tool for do-it-yourself script change is the *egogram* as developed by Dr. John Dusay.[15] The egogram is a graphic representation of the way a person divides his or her psychic energy among the ego states. For example, here is one person's egogram:

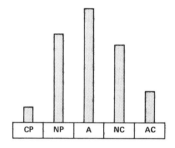

As you can see, this person spends most of her time in her three effective ego states and little time in her ineffective ones. She probably gets a lot done, enjoys life, and takes appropriate care of herself and other people. There is no single "correct" or "best" egogram—there's room for quite a bit of individual variation among people who take an "I'm OK, you're OK" position, and these differences help to make people interesting and unique.

A critical, prejudiced, childish person (like the television character Archie Bunker, for example) might have an egogram that looks like this:

59

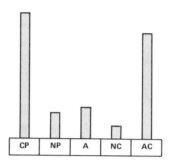

This person is putting so much energy into Critical Parent and Adapted Child that he has little energy left for his Nurturing Parent, Adult, and Natural Child. He therefore spends very little time in those ego states. People have only so much psychic energy with which to energize their ego states, and the egogram illustrates the fact that if someone is putting a lot of energy into one ego state, he will have less energy available to put into his other ego states. Dr. Dusay has noted that while people are "getting well" in therapy, their egograms change as they switch their psychic energy to their more effective ego states.

Anyone who has learned how to identify ego states can draw surprisingly accurate egograms of friends and associates. (By accurate, I mean that the egogram would be quite similar to those drawn by others who know the person, and perhaps even similar to one the person would draw for himself.) It's easy and fun to draw egograms because this is done through intuition rather than through specific measurements carefully plotted on graph paper. The actual length of the bars isn't important; the question is, which ego states are high, and which are low? The most accurate egograms are drawn by the Little Professor and reflect observations made by the Child. When drawing an egogram, therefore, it is better to do so quickly, without stopping to think about it. This helps to ensure that the information comes from your Little Professor instead of from your Parent or Adult. I invite you to stop right now and draw the egograms of two or three people you know well.

In all probability, though it may have taken you a minute to decide which was second, third, and fourth highest, you had little trouble deciding which were the most and least prominent ego states in each person. Now that you've had some practice, how about drawing one for yourself?

Are you happy with what your egogram shows? Or would you like to decrease the amount of time you are spending in Critical Parent and Adapted Child? If you would, all you have to do is increase the time you spend in your more effective ego states; in other words, to consciously use them more often. Because you have only so much psychic energy, this will naturally draw energy from the ego states you do not want to use. Making sure to use Nurturing Parent, Adult, and Natural Child regularly is much easier than trying not to use your ineffective ego states. You can do your own therapy by exercising your deficient ego states, which changes your egogram.

How can I exercise my effective ego states?

One way to develop exercises for your ego states is to watch people who have exceptionally high Nurturing Parent, Adult, or Natural Child ego states. What are they doing that shows they are using these ego states? What did you like to do when you were a little kid? Would anything along those lines appeal to your Natural Child today?

One man whose egogram showed a high Adult but very low Nurturing Parent and Natural Child noticed that two people he knew who had high Nurturing Parents were also excellent cooks. He did not know how to cook, so his meals at home were composed of canned and frozen foods. He decided to take a class in cooking in order to exercise his Nurturing Parent. To his surprise, he enjoyed the class. It led to his making much better meals for himself, so that he was far more nurturing of his Natural Child. He soon discovered that he enjoyed cooking for other people as well, and he began to invite friends to have dinner at his apartment. This led to more invitations from his friends, and therefore to more fun for his Natural Child as well. The cooking class, which was undertaken merely as an exercise for his Nurturing Parent, also served to strengthen his Adult (which became interested in learning about nutrition and the chemistry involved in food preparation) and his Natural Child (which not only relished the increased nurturing but also enjoyed the creative aspects of cooking and the social activities it generated). Thus a relatively small change in this man's activities (attending the class) led to a marked change in his egogram and improvement in several aspects of his life.

Chapter V

HOW DO PEOPLE PLAY IT CROOKED?

I've heard about "games people play." What are they?

Eric Berne's book, GAMES PEOPLE PLAY[16], explained his concept of psychological games and described a number of them that are commonly played in our society. A game is a series of transactions, often repetitive, with a predictable outcome, a hidden motive, and a payoff of bad feelings for the initiator and many times for the responding person as well. The purpose of a game is to get needs and wants met and feelings expressed. The intent may be okay; however, it is an ineffective and crooked way of carrying out that intent, and games are almost always destructive. Games also advance one's script and reinforce script decisions. Because games are not played with Adult awareness, the initiator of the game seldom realizes that he is inviting a crooked transaction or that he is saying one thing on the social (open) level and another thing on the psychological (hidden) level.

Games clearly have their origins in childhood. When a child does not get his wants and needs met in straight ways, he will often turn to games as a way to meet them. People often play the same games in adult life that they practiced and got good at in childhood. I, for example, traced my game of Poor Me back to the fifth grade, where I would do a song-and-dance routine about living in a poor neighborhood and would always be stroked for it. In adult life, I had a tendency to complain about working too many hours, and again I would receive a lot of sympathetic strokes.

Sometimes children learn to play games by observing their mothers and fathers interacting with each other. In other cases, children intuitively learn what games to play with their mothers, fathers, and siblings. When they find that the games get them strokes, they are reinforced to continue the games.

Games are based upon discounts. As we will see, it takes *two* discounts to play a game. The discount is a "put down" of my own needs, wants, or feelings, those of someone else, a problem, or the siutation. For example, a game can be initiated by a perfectly reasonable request that is ill-timed. How many times has a husband asked a wife to make love when she is irritable, tired or very busy? The result is that he is "rejected" and feels persecuted. Little does he realize that he has initiated a game of Kick Me by discounting the existence of a problem. Discounts are communicated through actions as well as words; a smile or an enticing maneuver can convey a discount just as easily as something that is said.

A game cannot be initiated without a discount on the part of the first player, and no game develops if the second person refuses to discount. In other words, there is seldom a persecutor or a rescuer without a cooperative victim. Each game has six steps: a con, a gimmick, a response, a switch, a cross-up, and the payoff. Here's a typical game:

Secretary: "I have to work late tonight, Mr. Smith."

This sounds like an Adult stimulus on the social level. At the same time, however, she makes some suggestive gesture with her walk, her eyebrows, her tone of voice, or in some other way conveys a sexual message on the psychological level ("Let's get sexy"). If Miss Jones is not aware that she has sent this message, she is discounting some of her own sexual feelings. If she is aware, and has no intention of following up on the message, she is discounting Mr. Smith.

This overt and covert stimulus is called "the con." The ulterior component is a secret stimulus from Child to Child, Parent to Child, or Child to Parent. In this case, it is a Child-to-Child stimulus, "Let's get sexy."

Boss: "I need to work late also."

This is his response to the overt stimulus. The game will not proceed unless he also responds to the covert stimulus. He probably will do so, however, because there is a "gimmick" involved, an area of weakness or vulnerability on his part which she intuitively perceives. In this case, the gimmick is that the boss does not have sufficient sexual self-control.

The con, plus the gimmick, elicits a response to the ulterior message: the boss thinks, "Boy, would I ever like to take you to bed!" and makes some overt sexual gesture. This is the second discount, without which the game would not take place. Mr. Smith is responding to a covert message without taking into account himself, Miss Jones, and the situation.

Secretary: (indignantly) "Why, Mr. Smith, I'm surprised at you! Just because I'm a secretary doesn't mean I'm a sexual object!"

This part of the game is called the "switch." The secretary is now denying her earlier, secret stimulus.

Boss: (confused) "I'm sorry, Miss Jones. I certainly don't think of you as a sexual object, and I apologize."

This is the "cross-up" in which the respondent, because of the switch, is surprised or confused.

The boss leaves, feeling guilty. The secretary feels justifiably angry (and has also reinforced her belief that "men are all alike"). She has won her "payoff" of bad feelings—in this case, an excuse to be angry. As in most games, the playee also ends up with a negative feeling (and probably with reinforcement of one or more of his script beliefs as well).

Why would anybody want to play a game and end up with bad feelings?

There are seven reasons for playing games: to structure time, to promote the script, to get strokes, to collect stamps, to make other people predictable, to avoid intimacy, and to promote one's basic position.[17] In my clinical practice I have found that most people, after they identify games that they play, are able to find out why they have been playing them by checking this list of reasons.

Usually a game will accomplish several of these aims at once. For example, people who play games around alcohol usually receive a tremendous number of negative strokes for drinking excessively. The amount of time they structure in drinking, having a hangover, having bad feelings, and discussing their drinking with people, is enormous. They have decided in childhood that they are not OK, and after every drunk they end up feeling very not-OK about themselves. Many alcoholics promote their scripts by drinking. The outcome of an alcoholic script is often death, or at least an unhappy life. When alcoholics drink, they are certainly avoiding the intimacy of which they are afraid. They can collect feelings of guilt, depression, and/or anger as results of each drinking episode. Last, they can make those around them very predictable because they know that each time they drink their spouses will be angry, disgusted, et cetera, and may wish to withdraw from them for several days. The Child wishes to make people predictable because it feels more comfortable when this need for structure is met.

Although the payoff of a game is usually a bad feeling, at least it is a *familiar* feeling. Sometimes there is a feeling of glee or justification on the part of the player. It is interesting to note that the player

65

often ends up with the same bad feeling he had when he started the game. For example, if Mom is mad at her son for doing something, she may start a game with him that invites him to lie to her. If he does so, she can then be angry that he lied, add this "mad" to the original mad, and be "justified" in expressing her anger.

In every game there is a Victim. There is also a Persecutor or a Rescuer, or both. Dr. Stephen Karpman made a great contribution to TA when he described these roles with the Drama Triangle.[10] This triangle is upside down and is based on a Victim position, meaning that there can be no game without a willing Victim. The arrows indicate that it is possible to switch to any position on the triangle (that's where the drama comes in), so that the person who enters the game in one position can count on spending some time in another. The Victim role is responded to by a Persecutor or a Rescuer—and sometimes by both. Any participant may end up having played all three positions on the triangle:

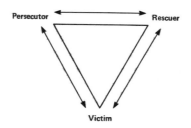

Persecutor   Rescuer

Victim

For example, in this game, Son is not listening to Mama. Mama begins to feel like a Victim who is being Persecuted by the boy. She calls Daddy to handle the youngster. Daddy, who is a Rescuer, rushes home and shouts angrily at his son. Now Dad, who was the Rescuer of Mama, becomes the Persecutor of Son, who in turn was Mama's Persecutor and is now Daddy's Victim. Mama, overhearing the shouting, rushes in and advises Dad to calm down and not be so harsh on the boy. Mama, the original Victim, is now the Rescuer of Son, the new Victim; however, Dad perceives that he is being victimized by Mama, who is Persecutor to him. The Drama Triangle is a clear illustration of the fact that anybody who participates in a game is likely to end up as a Victim. A good way to avoid games is to avoid playing any of those roles.

Most games are variations of Now I've Got You, You Son of a Bitch (NIGYSOB) and its complementary game, Kick Me. NIGYSOB is the most common game played in marriage and business. In this game, a person seeks to find others' errors and inconsistencies, only for the purpose of "catching" the person and not really to resolve the problem. For example, Wife comes home from work and notices that the house is in pretty good shape except that Husband has left crumbs and a knife on the kitchen table. She pounces on him for this.

He, on the other hand, invited the kick by leaving the knife and crumbs out, knowing full well that Wife gets very irritated about that sort of behavior.

Another example of Kick Me/NIGYSOB is one in which I participated. A close friend of mine would often invite me to meet him for breakfast at a given time. I would arrive on time, and he would be 15 to 20 minutes late. He was playing Kick Me, because he was aware that I get angry at his lack of punctuality. I played NIGYSOB by discounting the fact that he rarely gets to places on time. In any game between two people, if one decides not to play, it is not difficult to stop the game. (Remember, *two* people must discount in order to have a game.) Once I decided to quit playing the game, I asked my friend to call me as he was leaving home, so that we would arrive at the restaurant at the same time. End of game.

What can I do if I don't want to play games?

You can simply refuse the invitation to play a game. For example, I was having dinner recently with a couple who are friends of mine. He looked at me while he accused his wife of doing something, clearly inviting me to give my opinion on the matter. Just as she opened her mouth to defend herself, I stopped the game by saying that I really didn't want to get into that sort of discussion. I had recognized an invitation to play a game called Courtroom. This game is often played in business. For example, two subordinates who are at odds with one another come into the boss's office. One accuses the other of something and the other defends himself; in other words, one is the plaintiff and one is the defendant. The boss becomes the judge and jury. To avoid Courtroom, the boss does not become a Rescuer and instead invites the two people to talk *to each other*. He intercedes only in helping them to resolve their conflicts for themselves.

Another thing you can do to avoid playing a game is to expose it. Recently a person asked me for some advice on how to deal with his wife. I then made several suggestions. He responded to each of them by saying, "Yes, but I tried that and it didn't work." I recognized that we had begun a common game called Why Don't You...Yes, But. On the social level, WDYYB looks as if one person is trying to solve a problem by asking another person for advice. On the psychological level, however, the person is not trying to solve the problem at all. Instead, she or he is trying to prove that the problem is insoluble, and that nobody can help—especially the playee, who ends up feeling confused, hurt, or uncomfortable in some way. I exposed this game by pointing out what had happened and asking whether he wanted an answer, or merely wanted to justify his belief that his wife was impossible and nobody could help him with her. Another way I could have stopped this was in the first transaction: I could have begun by asking him what he has done already, instead of offering him suggestions like an omniscient Rescuer. A third way of avoiding the game would have been to suggest that he develop some possible solutions for his problems and to indicate that I would then help him decide for himself which one to follow, rather than propose solutions and give him advice. (A client of mine once gave me a sign that said, "A piece of advice... don't give it.") I could have crossed transactions by being Adult instead of Rescuing his Adapted Child.

Sometimes it can be effective to recognize a game and go along with it consciously, for the purpose of inviting the initiator to look at what happened and to learn from the experience. I had a client who would come to a therapy group and sit passively while the other group members worked. Then, when the session was almost over, she would finally ask for assistance, knowing that there wouldn't be time to get it. She could play Poor Me because she was deprived of help, or NIGYSOB because I didn't see to it that she got what she needed. In a therapy session, I pointed out the game to her. I showed her that she initiated the game by asking for help when there was five minutes left in the session, instead of at a time when she could expect to get what she needed. I also pointed out that she usually ended up feeling very bad and/or angry at me because I wouldn't give her the help that she wanted. It was important for her to play this game out in group, so that she could be conscious of a way she often plays out this same game in life. As a result of this experience, she agreed to ask for help during the first half of every therapy session and began to overcome her passive behavior patterns.

It is also possible to go ahead and play a game but refuse to give the payoff. Before I stopped the game with my tardy breakfast companion, I avoided giving the payoff on several occasions by simply deciding not to feel bad about his being late and deciding not to kick him.

What happens if I just stop playing a game?

When you refuse to play a game with someone who is used to playing with you, that person is likely to respond in one of several ways. He may play the game harder, to see whether you really mean it; he may find somebody else to play with; or he may make some other response.

For example, a client of mine finally decided to leave her alcoholic husband if he ever began drinking again, and she told him so. He stopped drinking for a long period, but then went on a binge (played harder). She asked him to move out. At this point it looked as if she "meant it"; however, he broke his leg (played harder) and she decided to let him move back in with her.

A game-player may simply change games and try again. A husband comes home, feeling quite unhappy and frustrated about his job. He is in a Victim position, and what he wants from his wife is some understanding, although he doesn't ask for this. The wife responds, also from Victim, by complaining about how bad her day was. (They are vying for the Victim position.) At this point, the game cannot continue, because two people cannot occupy the Victim position at the same time, so he switches and becomes a Rescuer by telling her what to do about the kids. She is then infuriated because he is always giving her advice. In this case, when he didn't get strokes as a Victim in one game, he started another game in which he was a Rescuer to his wife's Victim, she switched to Persecutor, and he ended up getting the Victim strokes he wanted in the first place.

It is very common for a game-player to find somebody else to play with if you refuse to continue playing. This is often seen in the divorce-remarriage sequence where a spouse decides to be straight and not play games anymore. The husband or wife then decides on divorce because they are "no longer compatible" (i.e., the other person is no longer willing to play the familiar games). The husband or wife then marries someone who is very much like the old spouse used to be, so that the games can continue.

Sometimes a game-player will decide to quit playing games and be straight, to stop using ulterior ways of getting strokes and getting what she wants. This is more likely to happen if the game is exposed and both parties decide on more effective ways of dealing with each other.

The aforementioned options are very common. There are three other responses to refusal to play games that are much less common; however, we can read about them in the newspapers every day: if people refuse to play games, the initiator can go crazy, kill himself, or kill others.

Does that mean it's dangerous to stop playing games?

Ordinarily, it is not at all dangerous to refuse to play a game. I might add that it is understandable that a long-time game companion would be angry or confused when you stop playing games, because you've had an unwritten agreement for many years and now you wish to change it, unilaterally. In fact, you selected each other, in part, because your Little Professors knew intuitively that you could "do you number" with each other. You saw each other's vulnerabilities and weaknesses. For example, several years ago (not recently, of course!) I felt unsure of myself while giving a presentation. I didn't deal with my feelings but instead discounted them. I acted out my discomfort to the audience, in subtle ways. Throughout that morning I was the victim of comments by NIGYSOB players. They perceived my "gimmick" or weakness, I defended myself, and ended up getting kicked.

As I said before, it is seldom dangerous to refuse to play a game. If you are involved with a third-degree game-player, however, it is often a good idea to get professional help. Games are played in three different degrees. The first-degree game is played on a socially acceptable level, and the severity of the payoff is minimal. The second-degree game has a more severe payoff and very negative consequences. The second degree implies social unacceptability—usually, the participants would rather not have anybody else know that they are playing. The third-degree game involves physical or mental damage to one of the participants. This can include ending up in the hospital, the jail, or the morgue. The aforementioned boss-secretary Rapo game was a second-degree game. If it had been a simple flirtation, with the boss responding in a less overt, rather innocent way, she might have just invited him to buzz off. Such a flirtation could well have happened at a cocktail party, with other people hearing the conversation, and the payoff would have been mild for both parties. This game played at third degree might have ended up with the boss forcing himself on the secretary. She would then cry "Rape!"and press charges.

I may initiate games without being aware of this. How can I avoid doing so?

If you know how to initiate getting what you want in a straight, open way, you will not play games. We have discussed a number of principles that will help increase your awareness and get the strokes you need: crossing transactions when necessary; expressing your feelings in a healthy way; asking for what you want and expecting others to do the same; giving, accepting and asking for positive strokes; examining your childhood decisions and changing those that are ineffective; staying off the Drama Triangle, and so on. As you pay more attention to your communications with others, as well as to your needs, wants and feelings, your awareness of your own psychological-level messages will increase and you will be less likely to send messages of which you are not consciously aware.

Chapter VI

WILL I HAVE TO BREAK THE RULES?

If you are going to make the kinds of changes that will improve your relationships and your effectiveness on the job, it will be necessary to break a few unwritten rules of our society and discard certain common cultural beliefs. For most people, these rules and beliefs are "given"—so basic that they seem to be facts of life. We seem to "know" these things without having been told; actually, however, they have been taught to us and we have learned them through our own observations since the day we were born. When we uncover these hidden rules and evaluate them, when we submit these "facts" to Adult examination, we find that many of them are simply not true, that some do not serve society well, and that some are very damaging to us as individuals. Part of making things go better is to identify and drop those culturally transmitted rules and beliefs that are erroneous and harmful.

For example, there is a strong support in our culture for the insidious and destructive belief that other people can *make* us do things, make us happy, make us sad, make us angry. Many of us use such beliefs to justify remaining unhappy, "stuck," and ineffective. Another insidious "given" is that things "just happen." Many believe that they have little or no control over what happens to them. ("That's life." "It's fate.") But people *are* in control of their lives, whether they know it or not. They are creating their own happiness, their own misery, and their own destinies. Very often, people wait for things to happen *to* them instead of making things happen *for* them. Some people search for happiness as though they expect to find it under a tree somewhere, instead of creating happiness for themselves. Some people are sitting around, waiting for Santa Claus—or, as Eric Berne put it, they are waiting for rigor mortis to set in.

In reality, most of people's limitations are self-imposed. This occurs because we have bought into our parents' frame of reference about ourselves, about the world around us, and about how we will relate to that world. We have *decided* what we can and cannot feel, think, and do. Many of these decisions were valid in childhood, as ways of adapting to stressful circumstances. Unfortunately, we have simply hung onto them, even though they no longer have validity in our adult lives. We can free ourselves from self-imposed limitations by identifying these early decisions and changing them. Anything we have decided, we can choose to re-decide, and by so doing we can re-create our destinies.

You have the power to change your childhood decisions.

You are also in charge of how you feel. Just as you have the power to make yourself miserable by what you think and do, you also have the power to make yourself happy by what you think and do. If you'd like to experience your ability to create your own feelings, Robert Goulding has suggested this exercise:

Take 15 seconds to think about a negative experience you've had in which you were really feeling bad. Re-experience that feeling.

Take another 15 seconds to reflect on a very pleasant experience that you've had. Re-experience those feelings.

What did you find out? You may have demonstrated that you can create your own feelings, both pleasant and unpleasant. You may have just discovered that it is easier to create good feelings for yourself than to create bad ones. You may have decided that the exercise didn't make any sense to you, so you choose not to do it at all. If you did the exercise, you have shown that you have the power to create feelings within yourself and to change those feelings. In any case, you have demonstrated that *you* decide what to do and what to feel: you are in control of both.

If in fact people do create their own feelings, positive and negative, then why do so many people believe that *others* have the power to *make* them feel good or bad? The answer to this question again lies in the decisions we have made for ourselves as youngsters, in response to stress and to family and cultural modeling about thinking, feeling, and behavior. Common expressions such as "You hurt my feelings!" "See what you made me do!" "That really makes me mad!" "You make me so happy!" "You made me love you . . . I didn't want to do it!" "You're confusing me!" reinforce the idea that people are not in charge of their own thinking, feeling, and behavior.

Transactional analysis provides many sound concepts for helping people to consciously take charge of their own lives.

Here are some of the most basic:

OWN YOUR OWN THINKING, FEELING AND BEHAVIOR—AND NOBODY ELSE'S

This is the number-one concept in transactional analysis and in psychology today. The fact is that *I* don't "make" anyone think, feel, or do anything. I can't even make a two-year-old do what he doesn't want to do. Have you ever tried to "make" someone happy who didn't want to be happy? It's an impossible task. If I'm responsible for your happiness, your orgasm, your depression, then I carry a very heavy load. If I'm responsible for those feelings within you, then you are powerless to do anything about them and you have to wait for me to change them.

The fact is that *I* am responsible for my feelings and actions, and only I can change them. People don't "make" me think, feel, or do anything. Rarely do things "just happen" to me—I make them happen. I grant you that, when a car runs through a red light and hits me, that did in fact "happen" to me and was beyond my control. Such happenings are the exception rather than the rule, however, and even the exceptions are sometimes suspect.

Nevertheless, many people really believe that they have no control over what they do, think or feel. For example, a truck driver who was moving some furniture for me bumped into a parked car with his truck. He then pulled up and accidentally backed into the car again. His comment was, "Why does this always happen to me?"

When I invite you into OK-ness or not-OK-ness, you are free to accept the invitation or reject it. If I tell you sincerely that I really like you, you may say "Thanks!" and decide to feel good about it. Or, you may say to yourself, "What does he want from me?" Clearly, you can either accept my invitation or reject it. What if I suddenly start shouting obscenities at you? How you respond to this is your decision. It may be appropriate for you to feel angry. On the other hand, you might decide to be understanding of me, you might question my behavior from your Adult ego state, or you might make some other response. Once again, you can accept or reject my invitation into not-OK-ness. The point is that my stimulus is as destructive or as effective as you permit it to be. This is not to deny that external stimuli can be very influential. The most extreme example that I can think of relates to two prisoners of war who are being tortured for information. One prisoner *decides* to talk, because he would rather talk than be tortured. The other *decides* to remain silent, because he would rather be tortured than to talk.

Some people have criticized these ideas because they interpret them to mean that it's OK to say or do anything, without regard for others. On the contrary, it is precisely because I am responsible for my behavior that I use my Adult to relate to people in a sensitive way. I believe that all people have an inherent worth and dignity, as I do; I choose to treat them that way, and I expect them to treat me that way. Since I am willing to assume responsibility for what I do, think, and feel, this greatly increases the likelihood that I will relate to others in sensitive and effective ways.

Dr. Taibi Kahler has outlined four ways in which people refuse to own their own thinking, feeling and behavior.[18] These mistaken beliefs are the real cancer in human behavior; they underlie the whole spectrum of games and ineffective behaviors:

> I can make you feel good by what I say and do.
> I can make you feel bad by what I say and do.
> You can make me feel good by what you say and do.
> You can make me feel bad by what you say and do.

When I recognize these beliefs as erroneous, and recognize my responsibility for my own feelings, I will have accomplished a change in my thoughts which will lead to changes in my behaviors and feelings. For example, if I quit believing that I can make people feel good, it's likely that I will stop Rescuing people, and I won't end up with hurt feelings when they do not reciprocate.

I can change my ego states by changing what I think, feel, and/or do. I can use "ownership" words to change ego states: "I am angry at you" (instead of "You made me angry"). "I'm feeling sad" (instead of "It makes me sad"). "I won't" (instead of "I can't"). "I want to" (instead of "I have to"). By using "ownership" words, I have moved from my Compliant Child to my Natural Child.

By thinking about how I feel, I can change my feelings and my behavior. I remember vividly how depressed I felt on a trip several years ago. I asked myself, "Self, why are you depressed? And when did it start?" I realized that I had felt "rejected" the evening before and, instead of sharing my feelings about the rejection, I had said nothing. I figured out that I had really been angry, and I therefore shared my anger with the person who had "rejected" me. Then I decided that it was important for me to get strokes for my Child, so I telephoned some friends and arranged to spend the evening with them. By thinking about my feelings and taking action to get what I wanted (strokes), I changed my feelings and experienced real warmth from the strokes I received.

What you *decide* is what you make happen. Not all these decisions were made in childhood: they are also made from moment to moment. It's not that I *can't* show feelings, it's that I *decide* not to in a given instance. It's not that I *can't* go up and touch people, it's that I *decide* not to touch them. It's not that I'm *unable* to confront someone who discounts me, it's that I *choose* not to do so.

Define your own OK-ness, and don't allow others to define it for you. Only *I* can decide that I'm OK or not-OK—no one else can decide this for me. I *am* OK; my *behavior*, however, is sometimes OK and sometimes not-OK. I am willing to hear and evaluate constructive criticism. If I decide that my behavior is not OK (that is, if I am discounting myself or someone else), then I am willing to change it.

Many people are overly concerned about possible rejection by others. Most of the time, what they are really fearing is that someone else's Critical Parent will try to make them not-OK. As a matter of fact, when I make *myself* not-OK I do it with my own Critical Parent. I recommend that you tune out all the Critical Parents in the world, including your own, and that you do not permit your OK-ness to be up for grabs. After you have decided that you are OK, you will have little to fear from the Critical Parents of others. Several years ago at a party, I spent a half-hour conversing with a lovely young woman. She was responding in a way which I thought indicated that she liked me. She asked to be excused, saying that she would return shortly, but she never did. If my OK-ness had been up for grabs, I would have felt not-OK and depressed or hurt. Instead, I evaluated my behavior as to whether it had been appropriate or inappropriate. I decided that her failure to return was not a result of my behavior; consequently, I felt irritated at her for a moment and continued to feel OK about myself. It was obvious to me that the *real* problem was that the lovely young lady had very poor judgment.

STAY IN THE HERE-AND-NOW

The concept of "staying in the here-and-now" was borrowed from the Gestaltists. If I stay in the here-and-now, it isn't likely that I'll get into gamy behavior. Unfinished feelings about the past tend to distort my ability to be objective about the present. If I am still angry at my mother for how she treated me when I was a child, I will tend to transfer this anger to people who are now in a position of authority over me. In addition, I can make myself not-OK by thinking such thoughts as, "If only I had done such-and-such," or by sitting around and hoping for the big break that will come in the future. All too often, I have driven through the beautiful Rockies and did not enjoy them because I was thinking about what I had to do when I reached my destination. Again, I was in the future, in another place, instead of in the here-and-now.

If I hold on to the past or worry about the future, I am wasting my psychic energy. How many people do you know who continue to mull over incidents that occurred a long time ago, or who continue to feel depressed about a loss that is many years old? How much energy do you waste on staying angry at a relative? Do you remember the sleepless nights when you agitated about what you would do the next day if your boss confronted you about something?

Finish up the past so you can live in the here-and-now. If you're still angry at someone, living or dead, I recommend that you either decide to give up the anger or decide to work it through. You may wish to write a letter, or to confront someone face-to-face. In Gestalt therapy, people finish up old "mads" and losses by imagining that the other person is sitting in an empty chair, in the here-and-now. They then express their feelings to that person and say whatever they need to say to resolve the old conflict. This process completes the past and allows the person to engage effectively in the present.

The Gestaltists use a technique that invites a person to get into the here-and-now: If I am feeling guilty, or if I am worrying about something, I can get in touch with what I'm feeling, thinking, sensing, and say this out loud; for example, "I'm aware of the sound of the air-conditioning, I'm aware of the tenseness in my toes, I'm aware of the bright sunlight," and so on. This process enables people to change ego states and to experience the here-and-now.

To have a thoughtful, plan-ful approach to the future is certainly productive; however, to worry about the future—or long for it to arrive—is to nobody's advantage. To remember the mads, sads, glads and scareds of the past is understandable, and sometimes enjoyable, but to invest a good deal of energy in re-experiencing bad feelings is destructive. Attempts to escape painful situations through preoccupation with the past (or the future, or another place) will only exacerbate the present problems; paying attention to here-and-now experience will help to solve those problems.

ASK FOR WHAT YOU WANT, AND EXPECT OTHERS TO DO THE SAME

Presenting a problem is not the same as asking for what you want. For example, if I say, "I'm hungry," that's a statement of fact, not a request for food. "Will you make me a sandwich?" is a request for food. I'm asking for what I want. Likewise, it is important to expect others to ask for what they want. When you give people something they don't want, they probably won't take it; in fact, you and they will probably end up feeling angry. For example, I come home from work, after a miserable day at the office, and tell you about my problems with the boss. I want you to understand my problems and comfort me, but I don't say so. Although I don't ask for advice, that's what you give. I am then mad at you for giving advice instead of understanding, and you are mad at me for not appreciating the advice. In this situation, one person expects the other to know what he wants. Very often, in close relationships, a person will expect the other to know what he thinks, feels, and wants—he expects the other person to be a mind-reader. The two are symbiotic and can crawl into each other's heads. It is far more sensible to *ask* if you want to know something, and to make clear what your wants are by making direct requests, instead of assuming that you know what's in someone else's head and vice versa. (To "assume" is to make an "ass" out of "u" and "me.")

Some people define reality on the basis of their wants and needs. They fail to consider the situation and the other person's wants and needs. If they want something, they believe that others should automatically acquiesce to that, whether or not the want is realistic. For example, I may know that my wife is tired and is not feeling well, but I want to make love and am incensed if she doesn't greet the idea with enthusiasm. I'll never forget that, in a similar situation, my former wife responded to me by saying, "Why don't you go into the bedroom and get started by yourself. I'll be there in a little while."

Another problem is that people often confuse their *wants* with their *needs*. Again, a *need* is something that I must have in order to survive; a *want* is not necessary for survival. I can tolerate not getting my wants met, but I cannot tolerate not getting my needs met. When people confuse wants and needs, they place undue emphasis on getting what they want and are intolerant of having their "needs" frustrated. In some instances, people really do believe that they will not survive if their wants are not met. Their confusion of wants and needs can lead to considerable distortion of reality. How many adults do you know who "need" their parents' approval in order to be happy? When they decide that they *want,* but do not *need,* this approval, they can create happiness for themselves, with or without their parents' approval.

People often have erroneous beliefs about wants and needs. For example, in an intimate relationship I may believe that your wants and needs should coincide with mine. If my want is different from yours, then I believe that yours is invalid, and vice versa. Also, I may believe that there can be only one valid "want" at the same time, either mine or yours. Or, I may believe that both of us cannot get our needs met—that one of us wins and the other loses. This is not true; both wants *can* be met, and both of us can win.

Many people believe that their partners can and should meet all of their wants and needs. Consequently, both walk around feeling overloaded, jealous, and often stroke-hungry.

Some people say to themselves, "If I have to ask for something, it's not worth anything," yet asking for what you need and want is the surest way to get it. If I invited people to play dice with me in a game where they couldn't lose—they could only break even or win—almost everybody would play under those circumstances. When you are wanting something and you are not getting it, what can you lose by asking? Asking will ensure that you either break even or get what you want. The worst that can happen is that the other person will refuse the request. Many people fear refusal because they feel not-OK about themselves and see the "rejection" of their request as a rejection of themselves. Only I can reject myself—people can reject my requests, but they cannot reject me. When I ask for what I want, I'll at least break even, and more likely I'll win.

All too often, people expect other people to know what they want without being told. This poses many problems, certainly the least of which is the fact that mind-reading is an inaccurate science. I have heard many people say, ten years down the road, that they were doing a certain thing because they thought the other person had wanted it all that time. Unfortunately, their assumptions were inaccurate.

Another erroneous belief is that asking imposes an obligation on the recipient of the request. Often we forget that a request is neither an order nor a demand, and no one is obliged to feel uncomfortable about it. A straight request does not put the other person in a compromising position or place any burden upon him at all. On the contrary, it gives information and offers an opportunity for the recipient to respond in a straight way as well. If you ask me for something, I then know what you want from me and have a chance to respond to you freely, with a "yes" or a "no" if I so desire, or to make a counter-request, or to negotiate with you. Perhaps I can offer you an acceptable substitute, if I wish to do so. Your asking creates an opportunity for both of us to express ourselves, level with each other, get what we need, and increase the authenticity of our relationship.

I often hear the argument that "people will be insincere and will give me what I want only to placate me." It's true that some people are unaccustomed to saying "no" to a request and habitually discount themselves by complying when they'd rather not. Then, they may choose to feel imposed-on, hurt, or angry at you for asking. If you are concerned about this possibility, you can build a preventing factor into your request; e.g., "I want to ask you for something, but before I do, will you agree to respond in a sincere way, instead of giving me something you don't want to give?" If the answer is in the affirmative, you can then make the request.

I recommend that you ask for what you want and expect other people to do the same. The Schiffs (TA therapists at Cathexis Institute in California) suggest that you identify *two* people in your request—a "you" and a "me"—and that it be in the form of a question. This is a clear and direct way of asking for something. If I say, "My back hurts," I am not asking for anything. Even "I'd sure like my back rubbed!" is a non-request, regardless of the facial expression, tone of voice, or body language accompanying it. A straight request is: "Will you rub my back?" It fulfills the criteria of indicating clearly what I want, and from whom, and it is a question that can be answered in a straightforward way.

Unfortunately, most of us were taught as little children that it's not polite to make direct requests. Therefore, we politely state our problems and leave them hanging in the air, with the implication that other people are supposed to figure out: (a) that we want something; (b) that we want it from them; and (c) just exactly what it is that we want (mind-reading again). This leaves room for all sorts of misunderstandings and bad feelings. It may be one source of the myth that a request places a burden on the other person—clearly, when I make such a "non-request" I *attempt,* through an ulterior message, to dump on you the responsibility for recognizing and meeting my want or need. You may then choose to feel put-upon, not only because I'm expecting you to mind-read but also because you haven't figured out how to say "no" to a question that has never been asked. Another problem is that, if I inform you that "my back hurts" when what I really want is for you to rub it, and you respond with a sympathetic "Oh, that's too bad!" or "Why don't you see a doctor?", I can choose to get mad at you and decide that you're insensitive, uncaring, or both.

It would be difficult to overemphasize the importance of learning to ask for what you want. So many problems can be avoided by the simple expedient of making sure that your request is a question and that the "you" and "me" are both identified. This may take a little practice. The indirect approach is so much a part of our culture that many people believe they have made a request when they have only stated a fact. We often hear people say something like "I didn't understand what you said" or "I'm confused about this" and really believe that they have asked for information. Even in trivial matters like this, I strongly suggest that you take note of such speech patterns and change them. For example, instead of the above, you could say, "Will you tell me what you said?" or "Will you explain this to me?" Requests that include a "you" and a "me" are efficient ways of contracting to get things done and of avoiding misinterpretations, evasions, and bad feelings. Stating requests directly may feel awkward at first, but it becomes easy with practice. After doing it a few times and seeing that it worked, I soon became quite comfortable in making my requests directly.

People often overadapt to what they *think* that you want. By mind-reading, they try to second-guess you and are often incorrect. A case in point was on my first date with Marilyn. In the restaurant, I was considering ordering chicken and began to think that Marilyn would view me as a slob if I picked it up with my fingers. Through attempted mind-reading I had decided that she wanted me to eat with a knife and fork. Had I not stopped this distorted form of thinking, I would have ordered steak to please her imaginary want and, at the same time, would have discounted my Natural Child, who really wanted to enjoy that chicken. Unless you have good information from previous experience, or unless you are a professional mind-reader, it is ineffective to presume that you know what somebody wants. Also, people's wants do change, and it's to your advantage to check them out.

Avoid Rescuing. We've already defined Rescuing as doing for someone something he is capable of doing for himself and, in the process, discounting that person and/or yourself. Please note that, if I am doing something for someone that he is capable of doing for himself and there is no discount, the activity does not meet the definition of a Rescue. Rescuers are Critical Parents who are masquerading as Nurturing Parents; that is, the Critical Parent says, "You're not OK," and that's what a Rescue implies. For example, if I ask a four-year-old how old he is, and Daddy answers for him, Daddy must be thinking that the child is too scared, or too dumb, to answer for himself. Daddy is saying, "You're not OK," and the boy picks up this message.

The simplest way to avoid Rescuing is to let people know that you expect them to ask for what they want. Then, make certain that by complying with their requests you don't discount yourself or them. If you frequently ask me for transportation because you have been unwilling to learn how to drive, I discount you if I continue to drive you around, something it would benefit you to learn to do for yourself. If you could easily take a bus or taxi to your destination, and yet I cancel an appointment so I can drive you there because I don't want to refuse your request, that can also be classified as a Rescue; I can end up as Victim.

There are many ways of getting what you want. Perhaps the most satisfying is when people give to you spontaneously. Obviously, if this isn't happening, asking for what you want is more efficient than expecting others to figure out what you want. When making a request, it is important that you use your Adult to take other people into consideration. For instance, when a person is clearly not receptive to giving, it is inappropriate to ask.

Another way to get what you want is to *model* ways in which others can give to you. For example, if you would like to receive compliments, give compliments. I am not suggesting that you give solely for the purpose of getting. If you give insincerely, you are likely to receive an insincere response.

Many people get what they want by "performing"; that is, by doing something in order to get strokes. Performing is one of several positive ways to get strokes; however, if the only time I get what I want is when I have to do something for it, after a while I get resentful. It's OK for people to give to me just because I'm me.

Remember that *wants* aren't *needs*. If I don't get something I want, I'll still survive. It is therefore unnecessary for me to be overly concerned about meeting a particular want. If you say no to my request, that's OK.

We don't have to have the same wants and needs at the same time. If my want is different from yours, yours is still valid, as is mine. We can compromise instead of it having to be my way or your way. For example, I want to go bike-riding this afternoon, and you want me to stay home with you and the kids. We have various options for compromise: I can ride for only half the afternoon, I can go riding today and do what you want tomorrow, I can take the family with me, I can delay my gratification and go bike-riding another time, without feeling "put-upon." It is important to our relationship that I learn to be invested in what you want as well as in what I want.

No one can meet all your needs and wants. One of the biggest problems in intimate relationships is the belief that one person can meet all of another person's wants and needs. There are many sources of stroking and need-gratification besides your intimate relationship—for example, your children, your job, your hobbies, your friendships. I strongly suggest that you cultivate the rich resources for stroking that are available to you.

Chapter VII

HOW CAN WE GET THROUGH TO F

Communication is the essence of civilizatic
itself. (It's unlikely that reproduction, for exa·
place without some sort of communication.) ᵥᵥ
together they are exchanging information in some way, oₗᵤ
words. Facial expressions, eye movements, body positions, gestuₗ
and voice tones have far more impact than is usually recognized.
These non-verbal signals are harder to keep under control, and therefore often more indicative of our real feelings, than what we transmit
verbally. We may not even be aware of the messages we're sending
on these non-verbal channels. Others may not be consciously aware
of them either, but nevertheless they get the message. If what we are
saying doesn't match what we are doing, others can sense this and,
as in an ulterior transaction, respond to the psychological-level message. If we're not aware of the messages we're sending on non-verbal
channels we may be quite puzzled by such responses: "Why did he
take it that way? That's not what I meant!" Except that's exactly
what some part of us did mean. If we are to communicate effectively
with others, therefore, we need to be in communication with ourselves. We need to be aware of our own needs, wants and feelings.

How do I get in communication with myself?

Self-awareness comes from use of Nurturing Parent, Adult, and
Natural Child, from an I'm OK-You're OK position. You can facilitate your internal communication by developing a strong, well-
informed, uncontaminated Adult ego state. Such an Adult has an
overview of your whole personality and is in charge of it even when
most of your psychic energy is in another ego state. This is called
"having your Adult in the executive position."

You can also increase your self-awareness by freeing your Natural Child, in the care of your Nurturing Parent. Effective parents
provide a safe environment for their children, one in which the children are free to enjoy themselves and express their feelings. When
your Parent takes care of your Natural Child in this way, it is easier
to become aware of your needs, wants and feelings because it is safe
for your Child to express them overtly. Of course, this does not mean
that your Natural Child can always have what it wants—this may be
unsafe, or even impossible—but it does mean that it's OK for your

to want it. Therefore, when you operate in Nurturing Parent, ...lt, and Natural Child most of the time, you are in better touch ...ith your Natural Child and this helps your communication to be clear, congruent and effective.

Is there anything that can make this easier?

There are several techniques that not only stimulate the effective ego states of others but also help you to energize your own effective ego states. These techniques can be called "rules of communication," although they are guidelines rather than hard-and-fast rules. Thoughtful use of these guidelines, when they are appropriate, can have far-reaching effects.

Ego states have something in common with muscles: The more we exercise them, the stronger they get and the easier it is for us to use them. Following the communication guidelines causes us to energize our effective ego states. It also makes our communication more authentic.

What do you mean by "authentic" communication?

Authenticity in communication is the sharing of needs, wants, feelings and thinking in a way that is sensitive to the other person's needs, wants, and feelings. Authenticity occurs in Natural Child-to-Natural Child transactions (intimacy), Adult-to-Adult transactions (sharing of factual information) and transactions between Nurturing Parent and Natural Child. An effective way to create authentic transactions is to pay attention to the words you are using. This is not merely dabbling in semantics. When I take the time to pick and choose my words, I am *thinking*. Thinking engages the Adult ego state and helps keep it in the executive position, as described earlier.

But won't this mean that what I'm saying won't match what I'm really feeling?

Choosing my words carefully does not mean using words to hide my feelings. In fact, using the words suggested in the communication guidelines is more likely to express my feelings accurately than using words that are typical of my ineffective ego states.

Thoughts, feelings and behavior affect each other. If you change one, the others tend to change also. Thus changing your words (behavior) can change your thoughts and feelings, which in turn can lead to other changes in your behavior. In short, changing your

86

words can change your personality. It also invites other people to change their personalities. It is with this understanding of the power of words that this chapter focuses on sound rules of communication that I have accumulated from various sources. Many of these rules relate directly to the all-important concept of owning your own feelings, thoughts, and behavior, and no one else's. If I am responsible for your feelings, thoughts, or behavior, then you are powerless to change any of these. If I own mine and you own yours, we both have the power to change. Here's how:

USE THE WORD "I"

Say "I" when you mean "I." Speak in the first person (use "I") when you wish to express your own point of view or feelings, instead of using "one," "they," "you," "people," et cetera. Speaking in the third person often comes from Parent and sounds like moralizing. "I" personalizes your comments, and it shows that you take responsibility for your own ideas. "I" lets people know about your Natural Child, Adult, and Nurturing Parent, and stimulates their Natural Child, Adult and Nurturing Parent.

Will that make me sound impolite and self-centered?

Using "I" appropriately is not at all impolite, although some Parents feel that it is. Many parents, and the societal Parent, have told us not to speak in the first person because this somehow calls too much attention to us and gets other people to think that we are egocentric. It is not the use of "I" that has this effect, however. "I" has been made the scapegoat for the real culprit: the ineffective ego states that use the word "I." When I say "I" from Rebellious Child or Critical Parent, I am automatically saying that I am OK and you are not. This form of bragging invites other people to respond in a not-OK way. When I say "I" from Adult or Natural Child, for example, the effect is quite different. If I talk about my ideas, my thoughts and my accomplishments from one of my effective ego states, without demeaning myself or other people, this is authentic rather than objectionable. If others do object, it is usually their Critical Parent objecting, and that ego state will find fault with everything you do anyway. I decided quite some time ago to quit letting my own Critical Parent, other people's Critical Parent, or my thoughts about what other people are thinking of me, guide my behavior. I decided to let my effective ego states guide my behavior, and I invite you to do the same. I also decided to take credit for my own ideas and accomplishments. This seems especially appropriate in view of something I recently heard Ken Blanchard say: "If you don't toot your own horn, somebody will use it as a spittoon."*

SAY "I WON'T" INSTEAD OF "I CAN'T"

Instead of saying "I can't" or "I'm not able to," say "I won't" or "I don't want to." "I can't" implies that you have no control over what you do, and this is seldom the case. Underneath the "I can't" and the "I'm not able to" is usually an "I won't" and an "I'm not willing to." (I am not suggesting that this rule be carried to extremes. I am reminded of the little boy who called from upstairs, "Mommy, I can't..." and was interrupted by his mother: "Don't say 'can't,' Johnny. You can do anything if you try." Johnny replied, "Well, then, will *you* please come up here and put the toothpaste back in the tube?" "I can't" and "I'm not able" are sometimes appropriate, especially when physical limitations are involved.) Avoiding "can't" and "unable" reminds me that I am in control of my actions and that almost everything I do, or do not do, is by my own choice.

Occasionally, it's certainly OK to say "I can't" when it would be insensitive to say "I don't want to." For example, if someone invites me to his home, and I really don't want to be with him, it is sensitive to say "I can't" instead of "I don't want to"—but not as a cop-out. Perhaps we would both be better off if I would confront him about his behavior and give him an opportunity to change it. Possibly I would then want to be with him.

REMEMBER THAT "HAVE-TO'S" ARE BASED ON "WANT-TO'S"

With the exception of biological necessities (e.g., breathing, sleeping), "have-to's" are usually only "want-to's," and it is more effective to call them that. Replacing "have to" with "want to" reminds me that I am a free agent: even if the choices are difficult, I do decide what to do and what not to do. "I have to work" is based on "I choose to work instead of going hungry or going on welfare."

People who believe that they "have to" do things frequently rebel against doing them, even when they have created their own "have-

*Kenneth H. Blanchard, Ph.D., is a well-known author and lecturer in the field of applied behavioral science. He is Professor of Leadership and Organizational Behavior at California American University, Escondido, and at the University of Massachusetts, Amherst.

to's." How many times have you said, "I have to clean the garage," and then found some reason not to clean it? If you recognize that your "have-to" is based on a "want-to" ("I want to have a clean garage," for example), you will resist less and find no need to feel so put-upon. "I want to" keeps the power with me; "I have to" gives the power to some outside force.

AVOID SAYING "I DON'T KNOW" WHEN YOU DO KNOW

When asked about your feelings, wants, or opinions, avoid answering with "I don't know" if you do know or if you just haven't thought about it. Stop and consider your answer. If you've thought it over and really don't know, it's OK to say so. If you do know but are not willing to share your answer, "I'd rather not say" is an appropriate response. Save "I don't know" for those occasions when you are asked for information that you do not have. Some people hate to admit that there are any gaps in their knowledge. When asked for information, they will come up with wild guesses, uninformed opinions, redefinitions, inaccuracies, or almost anything other than a straightforward answer: "I don't know."

AVOID HEDGING

When you have a definite point of view, avoid such words as "I guess," "probably," and "maybe," because these usually mean "I'm not sure." If you're not sure, say so. People who are being Compliant tend to cover their rear ends by adding qualifiers to statements that need no qualification. This is the same as saying, "I don't want to be vulnerable. If I don't take a definite point of view, you can't hold it against me." Definite points of view invite others to state where they stand. Yes, there will be some Critical Parents who will not like your being so definitive; however, you are not in this world to please Critical Parents, even if you could.

REMEMBER THAT NOBODY CAN MAKE ANYBODY ELSE THINK, FEEL OR DO ANYTHING

This statement is often misinterpreted to mean that, because I can't *make* anybody feel anything, I am therefore relieved of any responsibility for the consequences of what I say or do to others. This is not true; I am responsible for what I say or do, and you are the one who decides how to respond to my stimulus. If I throw a hand grenade at you, you are the one who decides whether to run, to take cover, to scoop it up and throw it back at me, or to stand there and get blown up, but this doesn't mean that it's OK for me to throw hand grenades at you. When I own my own feelings, thinking and behavior, I am *responsible* for what I say and do. When I'm in an I'm OK-you're OK position, I believe that every human being has the right to be treated with respect. I therefore accept the responsibility for relating to others in a sensitive way, from Nurturing Parent, Adult, and Natural Child.

On the other hand, a stimulus from me is only an *invitation* for you to respond in a certain way. My stimulus may invite you to think, to feel, to be defensive, to be accepting, to feel not-OK, or to feel OK, but your response will result from what you do in your head with my stimulus, not from the stimulus itself. If I say, "I like you," your response might be to slough it off by saying to yourself, "He didn't really mean it." Or, you might smile and feel good about it because you think or sense that I do mean it. Or you might not have any feeling about it at all, perhaps because you are busy wondering about my reasons for making that statement.

It is important to avoid expressions like "I made you angry," "you hurt my feelings," "it makes me happy," and "I made him feel bad." Instead, say "you look angry," "I feel hurt," "I'm happy," and "he feels sad about what I said." In this way, you own your feelings and the other person owns his. You own your stimuli and are accountable for them. You also own your responses to the other person's stimuli.

It bears repeating that if you believe others are responsible for what you think, feel, or do, you give away your power and incapacitate yourself. Some people believe that they are who they are today as a result of what their parents did to them, or because of things that happened to them during childhood. Such beliefs keep them powerless. If, on the other hand, they understand that they have made a variety of decisions in response to OK and not-OK parenting, they have the power to change their destiny.

If you believe you're responsible for what other people think, feel, or do, you carry too heavy a load. Family members often burden themselves with such beliefs. For example, parents often feel responsible for the behavior of their teenage children. When their teenager gets into trouble, they blame themselves and see themselves as "bad parents." A newspaper columnist commented recently that anybody who thinks he is supervising a teenager is himself in need of supervision.[19]

There is a fair amount of truth behind that statement, because parents cannot possibly be responsible for everything their teenagers think, feel and do. Teenagers have already made many decisions about themselves, other people, and the world, and their behavior reflects those decisions, rather than the attitudes of their parents. Parents provide a great deal of information and experience for their children, but they do not provide all the stimuli their children receive and do not control the decisions their children make as results of their life experiences. As a child grows up, he becomes more and more responsible for his own behavior, until this reaches a point where it is inappropriate for his parents to berate themselves about it or to try to take credit for his accomplishments.

It is equally inappropriate to feel responsible if your spouse is depressed or has a bad sexual experience. Although you may have influenced your spouse's feelings, you are not responsible for them. In any situation, it is important to be aware of the kinds of stimuli you are sending and to accept responsibility for them. It is equally important to avoid taking responsibility for how other people choose to respond.

DON'T TRY, DO

There is a big difference between "trying" and "doing." "I'll try" usually means either "I have no intention of doing" or "I won't do the best I can because I won't succeed anyway." I sometimes believe that a certain company's motto, "We Try Harder," is why they aren't Number One. They are "trying" to be Number One. Have you ever "tried" to stand up, or to throw something to somebody? If you do this little exercise, you will soon realize that either you are doing it or you are "trying" to do it. Generally speaking, when you "try" to do something you will not succeed. Eliminating the word "try" in this sense is another way of taking control of what you do. Which sounds more effective, "I'll try to do it Monday" or "I'll do it Monday"?

KEEP IN MIND THAT IF SOMEONE ELSE IS MONOPOLIZING THE CONVERSATION, IT'S WITH YOUR PERMISSION

If you are quiet, it's not because of the talkative person in the group. It's because you choose to be quiet; you choose not to interrupt; you choose not to change the subject. Others don't monopolize unless you permit it. How often have you left a committee meeting or seminar believing that it was a waste of your time, or that you couldn't get a word in edgewise? Frequently you have contributed to this problem by not speaking up, not asking for what you wanted, not stating your point of view. When you don't speak up, you buy into games of "Ain't It Awful," "Poor Me," and "Now I've Got You, You Son of a Bitch."

USE THINKING TO SOLVE PROBLEMS AND RESOLVE CONFLICTS

Hoping, waiting, procrastinating, complaining, arguing, complying, rebelling, and finding fault with others are ineffective methods for solving problems and resolving conflicts. The Critical Parent *tries* to solve problems (usually by indictment or decree); the Adult *does* solve problems, by thinking and by promoting authentic communication. Here are some guidelines for problem-solving and conflict resolution:

(a) *Communicate directly*

In a group, talk *to* a person instead of *about* him; e.g., "I like your idea, Sue" rather than "I like Sue's idea." Just as some parents sit at the table and discuss a child as though the child were not there, some executives in top management meetings talk *about* a person who is present, instead of talking *to* him. This invites Parent-to-Parent discussion instead of Adult-to-Adult conflict resolution or Child-to-Child creativity.

Failure to communicate directly is part of the game of Courtroom. In Courtroom, two people bring their problem to the boss. These two people do not talk to each other. Instead, the "plaintiff" tells the boss about the other person's behavior, and the other person defends to the boss, who is to be their judge and jury. The boss can avoid buying into this game by inviting the two individuals to talk directly to each other, by declining to take sides or make judgments, and by intervening only in ways that promote resolution of the problem.

(b) *Use eye contact*

Look at the person, make some eye contact, talk directly to him. This gives him recognition and enhances your effectiveness. Eye contact is an important mode of non-verbal communication, and it is often a good indicator of which ego state is operating. Infants withdraw from their mothers by breaking eye contact. The Rebellious Child and Compliant Child ego states tend to do the same thing. Critical Parent tends to look down from above; Compliant Child tends to look up from below. A comfortable, level gaze helps to maintain the Adult ego state. This is not to say that we should stare at each other when we talk; that would be both difficult and uncomfortable. Some eye contact, however, personalizes the communication and invites effective transactions.

(c) *Avoid questions unless you really want information*

Often questions are an indirect way of making statements; e.g., "Don't you think that ...?" instead of "I think that ...." It is more effective to simply state your point of view. Especially avoid "why" questions, because they often come from Critical Parent or Adapted Child. Other kinds of questions (such as "how" or "what") are more effective in eliciting useful information, in part because they are less likely to stimulate an ineffective ego state. "What are your reasons for doing it this way?" usually works better than "Why are you doing it this way?"

Asking questions is often an adapted way of covering your rear end or inviting a game. When mothers or employers ask "why," they don't always want to hear reasons. More often than not, they're angry and are just not leveling with their unhappiness. They would be better off saying "I'm really unhappy with you for doing X" instead of asking "Why did you do X?" Or, better yet: "I'm angry at you for doing X, and this is what I would like you to do instead."

(d) *Answer questions directly, and expect direct answers*

If someone asks you a question, answer it directly. Questions are often an area of difficulty in communication. Often the person who is questioned gives no response, or a response so vague that no answer is apparent; sometimes she answers what she thinks was "really" asked instead of what actually was asked. At

93

other times, she will simply answer a different question, one that she wants to answer. This is "redefining." People who redefine tend to answer a "what" or "why" question with a "who," "when," or "where," or vice versa. Kids are expert at this. If you ask Tommy, "Who made this mess?" he might answer, "I was out playing," which is answering "where" and not "who." If I ask you whether you enjoyed a certain conference, you might respond by saying that the food was good, or that you thought it was interesting, neither of which really answers the question. Sometimes a bit of evasion may be necessary in order to make a sensitive response. Please make sure, however, that you're really being sensitive and not just copping out when you respond as if you were a politician. How often have you heard people in public office, when asked about a given policy, respond by moralizing, and by being for motherhood and against sin, instead of answering the question? Have you noticed that I sometimes ask "How often?" when I am not interested in finding out "how often" and simply want to point out that something happens frequently? That's a violation of the preceding guideline, and it's from my Adult. I am inviting you to recall certain phenomena you may have noticed in other contexts and connect them with the material I am presenting here. There may be more effective ways to make that invitation, and when I find something that works better I may stop asking rhetorical questions; meanwhile, they are useful. The point is that I use my Adult to decide whether a guideline is appropriate in a given situation, rather than making these guidelines into Parent "rules." My Little Professor can be helpful in making such decisions. All of these communication guidelines are used most effectively by the Adult, often with the help of the Little Professor.

(e) *Don't assume, ask!*

Perception-checking and paraphrasing are extremely helpful tools for dealing with such problems as ulterior transactions and transferences. With perception-checking and paraphrasing, you can make sure that you are hearing what's being said and that others are understanding your communication. This is done by restating the other person's message, in your own words and in a different way, to find out whether you are receiving it as she intends. If you are not, she can then clarify her message. An example of perception-checking is: "It sounds to me as if you are saying that.... Am I correct?" If you want to know whether the other person is getting your message, ask her to paraphrase what you have said: "Please tell me, in your own words, what you heard me say." It is important that you ask others to paraphrase what you have said, because they can repeat your exact words without understanding your meaning.

(f) *Avoid interpretations*

An interpretation is telling someone what's going on in her head, what motivates her, why she is acting in a certain way, or how she feels; e.g., "You said that because ...." or "What you really mean is ...." Sometimes interpretations are a way of stating your own thoughts or feelings and disguising them as the other person's; for example, "The reason you have a frown on your face is that you're mad at me." The opposite is often true: "The reason I have a frown on my face is that I'm mad at you." Instead of interpreting, do the following:

(1) Inform the other person's Adult that you wish to check out your perception: "I want to check this out."

(2) Use your Adult to give a factual, unexaggerated description of the behavior in question: "You came home ten minutes late, left the door open, dropped your books, and raised your voice."

(3) After sharing your behavioral observations, inquire about your impression rather than stating it as a fact: "Are you angry?"

Interpretation is a common cause of conflict. Instead of dealing with behavior that people can see and hear, many of us mind-read in order to decide what motivates others and what thinking or feeling lies behind what others say or do. Since none of us mind-reads that well, we are much better off to state what we have seen or heard and ask the other person to interpret his own behavior.

(g) *Take into account feelings as well as thoughts*

When problem-solving, get in touch with and express your own thoughts and feelings, take into consideration the other person's thoughts and feelings, and make sure that the problem or disagreement has been clearly identified by both of you. You can acknowledge the other person's feelings even if you don't agree that those feelings are appropriate: "I understand that you're angry at me for not calling you. The reason I didn't call you is . . . ." The fact that you disagree with someone's point of view, or don't experience the same feeling, does not invalidate that persons thoughts or feelings. It's important to let the other person know that you recognize his thoughts or feelings, whether or not you happen to share them. This is essentially the opposite of discounting. Problem-solving is greatly facilitated when you take into account yourself, others, and the problem itself.

(h) *Focus on solving the problem*

In disagreements, people often focus on "winning" or "losing" instead of on solving the problem. When there is conflict, focus on finding ways you can *both* win through solution of the problem. This often necessitates compromise: "I know you want me to stay home this afternoon; since I wish to go, I'll go for only half the afternoon." Focusing on the problem helps avoid a competitive frame of reference. People who are being competitive are not particularly invested in solving problems; they are much more invested in proving that they are right and the other person is wrong, and in getting what they want regardless of the cost to the other person. Consequently the problem-solving session becomes a debate in which the other person is not acknowledged and often is not even heard.

(i) *Avoid giving false reassurances*

Say that the job market is very tight and your friend says to you, "I feel scared because I can't find a job." If your response is simply, "Everything will be OK, you'll find a job," that is a false reassurance that discounts the situation and your friend's thoughts and feelings. Such a response communicates that you don't really understand the situation, aren't willing to deal with it, or don't really care what is happening to the other person. Even if you do really believe that she will soon find a job, recognize her feelings first. Begin by letting her know that you understand how she feels: "I understand that you feel scared. It's difficult to be out of work."

People often give false reassurance in an attempt to "be kind" to others, because they think that those people are feeling too much pain to be able to handle the situation. The most efficient way to help people through a painful crisis is to help them deal with the feelings by experiencing them, expressing them, and finding that you do hear and understand. You can then help them focus their Adult on solving the problem. False reassurance frequently invites people to do nothing about solving their problems, to simply sit around being miserable and hoping that something will change.

(j) *Avoid exaggeration*

Avoid exaggerating the problem, what's going on inside you, or what's going on inside the other person. Use your Adult to assess the facts and describe them accurately. Expressions like "you always," "you never," and "I was so mad I couldn't think" are exaggerations. When describing what is going on, be factual instead of accusing or defending.

People who have a tendency to exaggerate often do so because they think that this is the only way they will be heard. This was their experience in childhood. They had to exaggerate in order to get Mom or Dad to hear what they were saying. As a result, they now exaggerate habitually and with little or no awareness that they are distorting the facts.

In learning these guidelines, you may find it helpful to concentrate on one each day until you have had an opportunity to practice all of them. You may want to write the day's guideline in your calendar, or jot it down on an index card that you keep where you will see it several times during the day. It doesn't take long for these patterns of communication to become second nature, and for the benefits of using them to become apparent.

I would like to offer special thanks to Dr. Leone Fine, Ph.D., Director of Seminars in Group Processes, for sharing so many ideas with me. Much of the content in this chapter was inspired by some of Dr. Fine's ideas.

Chapter VIII

HOW CAN I HELP CREATE CHANGE?

There are a number of ways for facilitating change. Confrontation is one of the most effective.

What is confrontation? It sounds pretty unpleasant

According to Webster, "to confront" means "to face, especially in challenge; to oppose." The word "confrontation" often carries negative connotations of discord, hostility, and even potential violence; "nice people" might be reluctant to confront in that sense. In TA, however, confrontation is defined as a positive act which benefits both parties through the sharing of feelings and information. In fact, if done with sensitivity, it is an act of intimacy. Confrontation is a process through which I can point out to you a way in which you are discounting me, yourself, others, or the situation. This pointing-out keeps our communication straight and clean, prevents the accumulation of negative feelings, and increases the probability that both of us will get our needs met.

It is true that I am OK as a person, and so are you. It is also true that OK people periodically do not-OK things; that is, they engage in not-OK behavior. What needs to be confronted, therefore, is behavior.

When I confront, I point out what I perceive to be a discount. When people put themselves down, fail to take into account the needs, wants and feelings of other people, or fail to recognize the existence or importance of a problem, they are discounting. I'm aware that I may do some discounting from time to time, and that I must be willing to confront myself and be confronted, as well as to confront other people.

What kind of things do I confront?

The confrontable behaviors that will be described in this chapter are manifested predominantly by Critical Parent, Rebellious Child, and Compliant Child ego states. I am simply delineating the variety of not-OK behaviors that these ego states tend to display. I would also like to remind you that people engage in not-OK behaviors primarily because their Natural Child is being discounted; that is, they have wants that aren't being dealt with effectively, or feelings that aren't being expressed appropriately. Instead of doing something to correct the situation, or to express their thoughts and feelings, they react with a variety of ineffective behaviors that are designed to cope with the situation rather than change it. These coping behaviors are usually not-OK and often warrant confrontation.

Some excellent transactional analysts at Cathexis Institute have done a fine job of defining and describing a variety of not-OK, confrontable behaviors.[20] These include overdetailing, overgeneralizing, discounting, redefining, and operating from a competitive frame of reference. One way or another, these behaviors are a block to effective communication, to intimacy and to the realization that all people have inherent worth and dignity.

We have discussed *discounting* elsewhere, but the information deserves re-emphasis here because discounting is such a common confrontable behavior. Discounting is a distorted way of thinking, or not thinking, about something. I am discounting when I pay insufficient attention to a problem or refuse to acknowledge the existence of a problem. This may or may not be intentional.

There are four kinds of discounts.[21] It is important to note, however, that a discount doesn't always fall into one of the four categories: most discounts involve a combination of categories. One can discount:

(1) *The existence of a problem* - There is a high rate of staff turnover within an organization, and nobody pays attention to this problem. In fact, it has never been identified as a problem

(2) *The reasons for a problem* - An employee is chronically late to work and says she is late because of the traffic. She is discounting the reason for the problem. (The real reason she is late to work is because she leaves home late.) In another case, sales are dropping and the company is blaming the salesmen instead of paying attention to the fact that competition has increased.

(3) *The solvability of the problem* - This occurs when people believe that they can't do anything about a problem, or that nothing can be done to solve a particular problem; e.g., "I can't talk to my boss!" or "There is nothing we can do to increase the production rate in our department."

(4) *People (yourself or somebody else)* - When I have a

feeling or a thought and, without good reason, do not express it, I am discounting myself. When I want something and, without good reason, don't do something to get it, I am discounting myself. When the supervisor makes an agreement with a supervisee and then breaks it, the supervisor is discounting the supervisee. When the supervisee says nothing about it, he is making a second discount - of himself, perhaps of his supervisor. When one person interrupts another, that person is discounting, and when the person discounted says nothing about it, she is adding a second discount. Eleanor Roosevelt once said, "No one can make you feel inferior without your consent." She was talking about a double discount.

It takes two discounts to play a game. If the first person discounts and the second person confronts the discount, thereby not discounting himself or the other person, the game will be avoided. In fact, the variety of not-OK behaviors described in this chapter are a result of discounting. If one doesn't discount, these behaviors will not follow.

Sometimes there is a problem in determining whether a discount has really occurred. Discounts may or may not be intentional, and they may be defined differently by each individual. I may say something with no conscious attempt to discount you, and you may perceive it as a discount. Even after your confrontation of me, I still may not see it as a discount at all.

Another very common confrontable behavior is called *redefining.*[22] When a person redefines, he fails to respond directly to what is going on. Instead, he changes the meaning of what has been said so that it complies with his own definition of "reality." If asked a question, a redefiner will often answer a different question, one that he has created, and thus shift the focus of the conversation. This is often done so subtly that neither party notices the redefinition, though the other may feel that there is something uncomfortable about the communication. A question is answered, but not the question that was asked. Here's a common type of redefinition:

> Employee: "When will the bonuses be distributed?"
> Employer: "Oh, yes, I'm very concerned about the bonuses. I see them as a very important issue."

In this instance, a "when" question was answered with a "how-I-feel" answer. It is also common for a person to redefine a "who" question by providing a "when," "where," "what," or "how" answer, and so on. A way of dealing with redefining is simply to point out that you didn't receive an answer to your question and that you would like an answer. Another method is to repeat the same question, in a clear, Adult manner.

Perhaps one of the most difficult behaviors warranting confrontation is *passive-aggressive bahavior*. This form of rebellion (which was discussed in detail earlier) is an indirect and ineffective expression of anger, manifest through forgetting, procrastinating, and doing things differently from the way agreed upon. One of the reasons that passive-aggressive behavior is difficult to confront is that very often the person engaging in this behavior has splendid excuses for it and presents them in such a way that the person being discounted is not sure whether he is making a mountain out of a molehill.

Passive-aggressive behavior costs companies millions of dollars every year. Employees who agree, or silently assent, to do something when they *really don't want to* will often do it wrong, forget to do it, or procrastinate and even miss deadlines, They will call in "sick," waste time, etc. Who knows how much equipment is misused or damaged and how many orders are misplaced or carried out improperly by people who exhibit passive-aggressive behavior? If these people would take the invitation to be straight about their opposition or their anger, and if the employer were willing to hear and understand them (not necessarily agree with them), it's likely that their underground rebellion would diminish if not disappear. As in dealing with any rebellious behavior, passive-aggressive behavior can be confronted effectively from Nurturing Parent and/or Natural Child. (See the material dealing with Rebellious Child in the section on transactions).

Eric Berne identified the *gallows laugh* and *gallows smile* behaviors[23] that are often worth confronting because they indicate a discount. Berne noted that people laugh or smile inappropriately about their behavior when in reality the behavior wasn't funny. People often smile, or even laugh, about behavior that had painful or embarrassing consequences: "Boy, did I ever mash my finger with that hammer, ha ha!" Inadvertently, other people tend to respond in the same way, creating a *gallows transaction:* "You sure did, didn't you, ha, ha!" In this case, neither person thinks that inflicting a painful finger injury is funny, yet both are smiling and laughing about the behavior, discounting their real feelings.

The employee who tells his boss that he is sorry he missed the deadline, and at the same time smiles about it, is displaying a clear example of the gallows smile. Often the employer, at the same time, may smile as he accepts the apology, even though he may be irritated. Inadvertently, the employee is supporting his own not-OK behavior by smiling about it, and in the same way, the employer is also unintentionally supporting the not-OK behavior. The Adapted Child is doing the smiling in support of behavior directed by the Critical Parent. The gallows smile is often an indication that the Adapted Child is pleasing the Critical Parent. The employer's cover-up smile when he was irritated may be an indication that he is following a "Don't Feel" Parent message (he smiles instead of feeling). Sometimes the smile is indicative of a person wanting the recipient of the information not to feel bad, even though the person himself feels terrible.

When someone smiles inappropriately, it is important not to smile yourself, and you may wish at times to simply point out that you don't see the behavior as being funny. I have found it helpful, when confronting my own gallows smile, to ask myself what it means. By so doing, I have often discovered some of my own adapted behavior. For example, I noted that I tended to smile when someone told me about an unfortunate death that had just occurred. When I asked myself what the smile meant, I found that I was smiling instead of talking about my discomfort over not knowing what to say upon hearing the news. I then realized that it was OK to talk about my discomfort and that doing so would help me make a more appropriate response.

Games are confrontable. Detailed information on how to confront them appropriately is available elsewhere in this book.

At Cathexis Institute they have developed the concept of "competitive frame of reference" as a mechanism whereby people do not get their needs met.[24] "Frame of reference" is the way in which I perceive myself, those around me, and myself in relation to other people. In some families, the frame of reference is one of competition: family members are competing for things (such as strokes or OK-ness) that the family erroneously defines as being scarce. In such families, children are taught that there are limited numbers of wants that can be met and limited numbers of strokes that are available. In a family with this frame of reference, it often happens that many wants of family members are not met and that they begin to believe that if one person has a want, it is not all right for another person to desire something at the same time. There is often competition around "which one" in the family gets his needs and wants taken care of, since it is presumed that it is impossible for everybody to get what they need. Members of such families therefore don't learn much about compromising (getting what I want now and what you want later, or both of us getting part of what we want now and the rest of it later), and they do not develop the simple ability to delay gratification. In the same families, children are taught that their OK-ness is directly related to how they compare with their siblings and with others. Instead of describing a child's characteristics directly ("Joe is cute." "Suzy is smart." "Tim has red hair."), these parents tend to make descriptions in comparative terms ("Joe is *cuter than* Suzy; Suzy is *smarter than* Joe; Tim's hair is *redder than* Joe's"). Parents compare siblings with each other and with children outside the family as well. Parents also compare themselves with others. Depending upon their OK-ness position, they either win or lose in these comparisons: "If you have more money than I do, then you're OK and I'm not OK." "If I get something that you don't get, then I'm OK and you're not OK." Another manifestation of the competitive frame of reference is that in an argument, because I am competing with you, I will not argue with the goal of solving problems. I will instead argue to win, or to lose, depending upon my OK-ness position.

Competitive frames of reference are present within many organizations. For example, the president of a company may be unwilling to hire competent people for fear that their competence will overshadow his own. In other words, if an employee is competent, the president feels diminished and not-OK about himself. Sometimes supervisors do not wish to hire competent subordinates for fear that if they do, they themselves will no longer be needed. Within departments, competitive people tend not to say positive things to their peers because of their belief that if a peer does something well, this means that they themselves are not OK. In other words, people in a competitive frame of reference are making continual OK-ness judgments, based upon comparisons.

One of the best ways to deal with a competitive struggle is to first take into consideration your thoughts and feelings and those of the other person. Then, ask yourself, and the other person, "How can we both win? Where am I willing to give, and where are you willing to give?" You can then negotiate a mutually satisfying conclusion—or, at least, an effective solution. If it becomes clear that the other person is still arguing to win, as opposed to arguing to solve the problem, you can invite sound problem-solving by refusing to compete and continuing to bring up options for consideration.

When I confronted myself about my own competitiveness, I became aware of how absurd it was. Upon returning from a convention, I told several of my friends that I was a great therapist. They asked me why I believed that, and I said, "Because the people at the convention were poor therapists." I then realized, for the first time, that other people's behavior said nothing about me. I learned to switch my ego states internally and to tell myself to stop the comparisons because they were of no value. This does not mean that I have stopped learning what to do and what not to do through observing the behavior of others. It simply means that I am now evaluating their behaviors directly ("That was effective") instead of in comparative terms ("He is more effective than I am") and that competitive OK-ness judgments are no longer involved.

Overdetailing[25] is another confrontable phenomenon. When someone overdetails, he picks up on a small segment of the issue (perhaps a single word, phrase, or fact) and relates to that exclusively, missing the gist of the issue. A supervisor tells a supervisee that he is really unhappy with the supervisee because of tardiness for five days in a row. The supervisee, who tends to overdetail, responds by saying that he has been late for only *four* days in a row. They then deal with whether four or five days is accurate and miss the fact that the real problem is repetitive tardiness. It is advisable to invite a person who overdetails to talk about the general issue and avoid focusing on the specifics.

Overgeneralizing[26] is a confrontable behavior. When a person over-generalizes, his statements are so general or ambiguous that it requires a great deal of questioning to discover what he means. For example, a supervisee complains to his supervisor that the people in his department "aren't doing their jobs." (He does not specify which of the people, and doesn't state in what way they are not doing their jobs, nor does he offer any other clarifying information.) The supervisor then asks him what he means. The supervisee replies that they "don't communicate well." This is still an overgeneralization, so the supervisor continues his questioning, which can sometimes go on indefinitely. When communicating with someone who overgeneralizes, you can point out that he is generalizing and that specific information would be helpful. You can also ask questions about individual elements of the situation, questions designed to elicit specific answers that will help both of you to zero in on the problem.

To confront or not to confront?

When someone is engaging in confrontable behaviors, I have three choices: I can confront him, I can stop transacting with him, or I can accept the behavior. The choice I make is dependent upon several factors. When deciding, I will take into account the situation, my relationship with the person (if any), my own feelings, and the degree to which the behavior in question is annoying, dangerous, or harmful to the person himself. If I tried to confront every bit of ineffective behavior I see, I would probably get very little else accomplished and certainly wouldn't have much fun. If I chose to simply stop transacting with everyone who is engaging in confrontable behaviors, I would soon run out of friends and associates. If I decided to accept all behaviors without comment, I would discount myself and deny those close to me the opportunity to learn about my thoughts and feelings concerning their behavior and perhaps to change what they are doing. In reality, we cannot *change people* with our confrontations. People change themselves. We can, however, provide the kind of caring confrontation that opens opportunities for improvements in our relationships with others.

I confront when it appears that doing so may solve or prevent significant problems. I also pay attention to whether the issue is of importance to my Child. In general, if there's something in it for your Child, it's worth confronting.

How do I confront?

Confrontation is essentially the giving of *constructive negative conditional strokes*. Therefore, it is a more effective tool for encouraging change if it is included in the context of day-in, day-out relationships where people get plenty of *positive strokes* as well. When you get plenty of positive strokes from me for what you do, as well as just for being yourself, you are more likely to respond thoughtfully when I give you constructive negative conditional strokes. If, on the other hand, I confront you regularly and rarely give you positive conditional and unconditional strokes, you are unlikely to perceive my confrontations as constructive. In fact, you may experience them as coming from my Critical Parent and react negatively to them.

Before beginning a confrontation, it is well to check on several important issues. First, are you in one of your effective ego states? Confrontations from Critical Parent or Rebellious Child are seldom effective. Second, consider the place: Would it be better to make this confrontation in private? (That is often the case.) Would asking for the other person's attention in this situation be a discount? (In other words, does he or she need or want to be paying attention to something else?) If you perceive that a person will not hear your confrontation because of the ego state she's in, it makes sense to either invite her to switch ego states by crossing transactions, as described earlier, or wait until a time and place in which she would be more likely to give you the response you desire. Timing is very important in confrontation, and discounting the situation is likely to ensure that the confrontation "doesn't work."

It is often important to get a contract for confrontation before you begin. To do so, you simply ask people whether they will listen and respond to what you have to say. For example, if I don't like something that my supervisor does, at the right time and place I might say something like, "Sam, I'm wondering whether you'd be up for my sharing some feelings that I have about what happened yesterday. Are you?" or "I have some strong feelings about what happened yesterday, and I'd like to tell you about them. Will you listen and understand me?" or "I'm afraid that if I tell you I'm mad at you, you might fire me. Will you listen to how I feel, and not fire me?" Some people object to this approach on the grounds that sometimes people will say yes when they really mean no. If you are concerned about this, I recommend that you build a safeguard into the contract. For example: "I'd like to ask you to do something, but only if you really want to do it. I'm afraid you might say yes even if you feel like saying no. Will you tell me how you really feel?" If the person agrees to do so, you can then proceed to ask whether she is willing to listen to the confrontation.

One of my goals in confrontation is to flow with people's energy; that is, to tune in to what the other person is saying, communicate my understanding of what he has said, and come to some conclusion that is mutually satisfying. For example, say that Joe is angry at me because he believes that I have not really recognized his expertise and effort. I have not given him the strokes that he wants. As a result, he has been getting his strokes by subtly demonstrating his dissatisfaction. Joe wants strokes. He didn't get them for doing a good job, so now he's getting them for being late. When I realize that what he needs is acceptance, both for being himself and for what he does, and am willing to give him this, Joe is then free to use his energy toward a mutual goal that is good for the organization as well as for him and for his supervisor.

It is easier to flow with people's energy when I keep in mind that almost all behavior, no matter how negative it may appear, is motivated by some sort of positive intention. In the example above, the intention behind the behavior (to get strokes) was "good"; Joe was unaware of his intention, however, and his behavior was ineffective for getting the kinds of strokes he really wanted. Joe may not have been aware of the connection between his tardiness and his angry feelings toward me. In fact, he may not even have realized that he *was* angry at me. Nevertheless, his behavior communicated the fact that he wanted something he wasn't getting. When I am sensitive to communications such as Joe's, and value the positive intention behind them, my confrontations are far more effective.

During confrontation, it is helpful to focus on *what you want* instead of on *what you don't want,* to give people "do's" instead of "don'ts" (e.g., "Do purchase orders this way . . . ." instead of "Don't do purchase orders that way!"). A mother might say to a child, "Stay in the yard," instead of "Don't go into the street." Thus, instead of trying to stop the flow of a person's energy, you simply help him divert it in a different direction.

Another way of flowing with people's energy is to encourage them to present their point of view, while you listen carefully and objectively. When they are finished, you feed back your understanding of what they have said. Then, they know that they have been heard and that you understand their position, even though you may not agree with it. This kind of listening and feedback also makes it more likely that the other person will listen to and understand your point of view, and perhaps make changes as a result of your confrontation.

When confronting, I like to start with a light touch. Effective confrontations need not be serious or heavy. When someone comes to work late, I might call out to him, in a pleasant tone of voice, "Hey, Joe, you're a little late—please watch it." Often I am even playful in confrontation: "You interrupt me one more time and I'll bite you on the neck!" The best time to confront is *before* a behavior becomes seriously annoying or damaging, and *before* anybody gets angry about it. This is not always possible, however. Immediate anger is an appropriate response to some behaviors.

Is anger really OK?

As discussed earlier, anger is one of the four basic emotions; that is, one of the four feelings naturally displayed by infants before they show any learned responses to what happens in the world. For an infant, anger is a normal response to not getting what he wants. It is the same for me, as long as I am responding to here-and-now happenings: anger is an appropriate response when I am not getting what I want, and the straight expression of anger is OK.

Many people believe that expressing anger is not OK, and there are several reasons for this belief. As I see it, people's biggest hang-up about anger is based upon their experience of its *inappropriate* expression when they were children. There was shouting and name-calling, hitting, pain, tears, and possibly uncontrolled rage. When they saw people expressing anger in these ineffective ways, they concluded that anger is explosive, injurious, and hostile. On the other hand, some people think anger is not OK because they *never* saw their parents express anger overtly. When they saw people outside the family expressing anger, they would say to themselves. "Wow, Mom and Dad never act that way!" and decide that showing anger is not OK. Some religious teachings are misinterpreted to indicate that we should never be angry. Many people were punished for displaying anger as children. Others saw enraged parents hurting themselves and others, and decided never to act that way. No wonder these people decided that anger is not OK! What they didn't know, however, is that anger, the natural feeling, was not the real culprit in those cases. The problem was that people were expressing anger from one of their *ineffective ego states*. They were not expressing their feelings in straight, appropriate ways. Probably they had been holding in anger until they decided that some incident, perhaps a minor one, gave them justification for an explosive outburst from Critical Parent or Rebellious Child.

Why do people build up angry feelings like that?

People hold in their anger because their own Critical Parent tells their Natural Child not to get angry, or because they are overadapting to other people. Overadaptation is the process whereby a person attempts, through "mind-reading," to determine what people want him to do and then tries very hard to comply with these imagined wishes. He decides how others will feel, or what they will think or do, if he takes some action or expresses some emotion. As a result of his attempts to read minds, he may decide that other people will react badly if he shows anger about "little things." He therefore overadapts to them by holding his anger in and letting it build up until he is so angry that expressing his feelings is "justified." Then, all too frequently, he expresses this built-up anger from Rebellious Child or Critical Parent. Because he doesn't express his little angers appropriately as they arise, he ends up expressing big, old angers, inappropriately. Or, he may express his anger covertly, through "thoughtless" behavior, inefficiency, "mistakes," "accidents," illness, sexual problems, or coldness and withdrawal from other people.

The way to get rid of unpleasant feelings is to express them appropriately. Held-in feelings do not simply fade away; they are stored up for expression sometime in the future. Anger *will be expressed* in one way or another; suppressing it neither gets rid of it nor prevents its expression. In other words, *if you don't say it straight, you'll show it crooked.*

Can't anger simply be avoided?

Trying to avoid anger is like trying to avoid living. Frankly, I'd rather not be angry ever again in my life, and if I could make everybody like me and never be angry at me, I certainly would. However, as my friend Mort says, "Abe, you're living in Disneyland!" Since Utopia doesn't exist, I might as well face the fact that I will sometimes feel angry, and that people will be angry at me from time to time, for the rest of my life. I am therefore resolved to learn to handle my own anger effectively and to accept other people's confrontations of me in a healthy way. Anger can be a way of building up energy for solving problems. If we use this energy effectively, we can solve most problems that confront us. If we refuse to use our angry energy for solving problems, we channel it into creating more problems for ourselves. The energy is simply there, for us to use, and I choose to learn to use it in positive, effective ways.

An example of the effective use of angry energy occurred many years ago when I wanted to borrow some money. Because I already owed some money, several banks turned down my loan request. I got angrier and angrier at each refusal. Finally I used my angry energy to improve my life. I decided to change occupations so that I would never again be in a similar position.

How do I confront effectively when I'm angry?

When I'm angry, it is often because I'm wanting something that I'm not getting. I invite you to think of a recent incident in which you were angry, and then ask yourself, "What did I want that I wasn't getting?" Is it true that you were wanting something you weren't getting? If so, were you aware of this at the time? Were you wanting someone else to change? The next time you're angry, I suggest that you focus on *what you want* and how you can change what *you* are doing in order to get it. It is often true that if you ask for what you want in a more sensitive way, or confront people in a more sensitive way, they will decide to change what they are doing.

I have found several principles to be helpful for expressing anger in a healthy way. I pair authentic positives with negatives when giving constructive criticism; for example, "If you had handled that customer the way you usually do, I'd have no complaints." I also make sure that I'm expressing my anger from my Natural Child, and from an OK position. I tell people how *I* am feeling; I focus on myself and not on them. I also express my angry feelings by simply letting them out, instead of explaining them from Adult or smiling as I speak. If I let my feelings out in a healthy way, I will not show them in a crooked way. Another thing I do is to let people know *which* of their behaviors I am feeling angry about, so that they will have that information and can choose to change the behavior if they so desire. The choice is really theirs. Lastly, I ask them for what I want instead. I can do this from my Natural Child, my Adult, or my Nurturing Parent. Often it is not enough to say, "I want you to stop doing X," because this does not tell the other person what to do instead, or what you would actually like them to do. The confrontation would sound like this: "Mary, I'm really feeling irritated. You told me that you would have the delivery by 3 p.m. on Wednesday, and it's now Friday morning and I still haven't received the supplies." Sometimes, for added emphasis, you might let the person know what effect their behavior has had on you: "Since I haven't received the delivery, two of my staff are sitting idly by, and one of my suppliers is quite angry at me because I haven't gotten his delivery out yet." You can then ask for what you want, from Nurturing Parent, by

111

saying, "Please get the delivery to us as you said you would," or, from Adult, by inquiring, "Will you bring the delivery in the morning?" or from Child by saying, "I'd like the delivery as soon as possible."

What response do I expect from someone I've confronted?

It is not always necessary to expect an immediate response. In fact, one very effective way of confronting is to share your feelings, thoughts and requests in a way that does not necessitate any response from the other person. If your confrontation *requires* a response, the response is often defensive and you therefore don't get the desired result. One of the simplest ways of setting up a response-free confrontation is to contract beforehand for the person to just hear you and then think about what you have said, rather than make any response. His future behavior will indicate his response.

When you do want a response to your confrontation, it is reasonable to expect that the person indicate one of the following things: that he understands your confrontation and is sorry or is willing to change his behavior; that he understands what you are saying and that he wants to think about it and get back to you later; or that he understands you, disagrees with you, and is unwilling to change his behavior. In the latter situation, there may be room for compromise. If not, and if the behavior is sufficiently objectionable to you, you may decide to discontinue the relationship.

Though it is a reasonable expectation that people let you know what they are or aren't willing to do in response to your confrontation, I do not insist on this kind of response to an initial confrontation. If the person continues to discount after confrontation, however, it's reasonable to ask for an agreement for behavioral change.

What if my initial confrontation doesn't work?

If your gentle or playful confrontation does not elicit a response that is acceptable to you, you again have three choices: you can stop transacting with the person, you can simply accept the behavior, or you can escalate the confrontation. To escalate is to increase the energy, and perhaps the intensity, of the confrontation.

I am reminded of a crude but effective example of escalation. Do you remember the story of the mule who would not respond to directions from his owner? The owner escalated his confrontations of the mule, first by shouting louder and louder, and then by using his whip.

No response. Therefore, a consultant (expert mule trainer) was brought in The expert looked at the mule, then went to his wagon, got out a two-by-four and hit the mule a resounding whack, right between the ears. The astonished animal immediately decided to make eye contact with the trainer, and soon it was following instructions quite nicely. The trainer smiled and explained to the owner, "First you gotta get their attention."

Sometimes a simple confrontation does not really get a person's attention. Some people will not change their behavior unless they are really uncomfortable with what they are doing, or with people's responses to what they are doing. Because they are experiencing no discomfort, they may discount a low-level confrontation. Escalation is therefore required.

Sometimes escalation is necessary because the person's Child does not believe that you are serious about your confrontation. If a person has been relating with you over a period of time and has been continuing a certain behavior without effective confrontation from you, his Child may not believe that you really want him to change the behavior. Why should it? I am reminded of the pre-schooler who was asked by a teacher to stop a certain behavior. Sometimes the teacher was consistent in expecting the child to stop, but sometimes he was inconsistent and let the behavior continue without comment or consequences. The child therefore continued the behavior, especially when the teacher was out of the room. It was not until the teacher consistently stood by his expectations that the youngster quit "testing." The child could then relax because she understood that the teacher "really meant it."

Do you remember Joe, who received a gentle confrontation about being late? Let us say that Joe continued to be late. I would escalate the confrontation by sitting down with him, chatting with him about the time problem, and saying, in so many words, that I really expect him to be at work on time. This level of confrontation is usually effective with the average person. There are some people, however, who are invested in rebellious behavior and who will need an even greater escalation.

There are certain situations that will not be helped by escalation of the original confrontation. These occur when the confronted behavior is only a symptom of some other problem. In the two previous examples with Joe, I was dealing with "surface behavior"; that is, I was treating the symptom of being late as if it were the problem.

If Joe's tardiness had no hidden motivations, the confrontation would probably be effective. Even if his tardiness was symptomatic of something else, confronting the surface behavior might have some temporary effect. The problem would recur, however, because there was a deeper reason for the behavior that was not resolved by the confrontation. Let's illustrate this with an example. Say that whenever I get a small sore I put merthiolate on it and it goes away. This time I have a little sore, and I put the merthiolate on it, and it appears to heal as usual, but then it comes back. If this happens, I need to stop treating the sore in the same old way, since that isn't solving the problem. Instead, I need to find out what is causing the sore and deal with that. Often an underlying cause can be treated quite easily, once it is identified. Sometimes, however, more and more radical treatment is required. It is the same when the usual confrontations are not effective in "curing" a behavior. When a person continues the same behavior over and over, I must confront the issues underlying the behavior. In Joe's case, I would probably begin the escalation by sitting down with him, describing his behavior, and asking him what he thinks is going on. I might even be willing to give him some of my own impressions in the form of an inquiry. That is, rather than *tell* him that I think he has been coming in late because he's mad at me, I would *ask* him whether he's been coming in late because he's mad at me. If he replies that he is angry at me, I would ask what he's angry about and listen objectively to his explanation. I would then communicate that I understand his feelings. If I agree that his reasons for being angry at me are legitimate, I would tell him how I am willing to change my behavior. On the other hand, if I thought that he had misperceived or distorted what was going on, I would discuss this with him. In any case, I would negotiate with him for a solution to the problem. I may be willing to compromise if the situation warrants it. In constructive confrontation, the object is for *both* of us to win. After consideration of the underlying issues, it's likely that the other person will be willing to contract for behavioral change.

Let us say, however, that Joe continues to be late. I now need to decide whether to escalate further or to accept the behavior. Sometimes an employee is so valuable that I am willing to overlook certain of his behaviors. If this is so in Joe's case, I will drop the confrontation and let him know that I will accept his being late. If not, further escalation is required—with consequences. In the next confrontation, I will identify what consequences there will be if Joe is unwilling to change his behavior. Consequences might even include termination. It would sound like this: "Joe, we've discussed the issue of your being late on several occasions. You know that when you are late, other people can't do their work effectively. We really need for you to be here on time." (Please note that the supervisor is making an Adult judgment about the importance of punctuality, versus a Parent value that "people should be at work on time." The supervisor might be willing to accept Joe's behavior if there were no significant Adult reasons for insisting that he change his behavior.) "I've come to the point where I am seriously considering termination. However, I'd like you to decide whether you are going to continue working here, rather than make the decision myself. If you wish to continue your employment here, then you must make a decision to be at work on time. If you decide to fire yourself, then you'll come to work late. Joe, I feel so strongly about this that I'd like to give you a half-day off to think about it." If supervision is done well, supervisors do not fire employees. A good supervisor never has to fire anybody. Instead, he enables employees to experience the natural consequences of their behavior. He tells them clearly what the job requires and what it takes to keep the job. If they then decide not to do those things, their own behavior fires them.

It is important that supervision involve giving people an adequate opportunity to change, with lots of direction and support in making those changes. A final evaluation should contain no surprises, nor should termination be a surprise. The decision to terminate is the employee's own.

These concepts are equally useful when disciplining or setting limits for children. They can decide for themselves whether they want to experience the consequences of their behaviors, after those consequences are clearly explained, or whether they want to change their behaviors instead. It is helpful for children (as well as for adults) to understand that consequences are directly related to their behavior. Otherwise, it is easy for them to think, "You did this to me!" and not realize their own responsibility for what has happened.

When do I stop confronting?

Certainly I want to help people change their behavior toward me when I find it unacceptable. I also think it's reasonable to expect my friends, relatives, and business associates to treat me with the same consideration I have for them. It may be to my advantage, however, to stop escalating my confrontation of a certain behavior when it becomes clear that the person is not going to change it short of consequences that might threaten our relationship. If the positives of the relationship outweigh the negatives, I may decide to stop confronting and accept the behavior.

It makes good sense to use my Adult to decide how much energy I'm willing to invest in a confrontation. I ask myself, "Is it worth it to me to continue? If so, how far am I willing to go with this confrontation?" One factor to be considered is the other person's investment in changing. This I can sense, and even quantify, from his responses. To expect complete and immediate change is unrealistic, but are the discounts now less frequent and less intense? If so, it might be worth continuing the confrontation until the matter is resolved. When the person refuses to change his behavior, I have a decision to make: am I willing to adjust to his discounts, and can I still feel OK about myself and continue to function well in this situation? Or does it make more sense to end the relationship? This guideline is applicable to marriage and divorce, as well as to employment and termination.

What are the pitfalls to watch for?

When people confront other people, they often tend to make the issue bigger than it really is. They do this either by getting madder than the situation calls for, or by talking about more than the particular incident they are confronting. This is because they have been "stamp-collecting." They bring to the confrontation old issues that they didn't talk about at the time, and the bad feelings they failed to express. "Stamp collectors" save up their bad feelings in order to justify their right to express them. They learned this little maneuver in childhood, when it was not all right to express how they felt unless they had damned good reason. You can avoid making issues bigger than they are by confronting small issues appropriately as they arise and by making certain that your anger is based upon here-and-now situations rather than on historical happenings.

I invite people to learn from the past and plan for the future, rather than dwell on the past and worry about the future. The security of the future is in the stability of the present. One of the practical problems in bringing up issues or incidents that occurred some time ago, even if only yesterday, is that people rarely agree on what was or wasn't said or done in the past. They then waste their energy talking about these disagreements instead of about the issues at hand. A

116

simple way of getting into the here-and-now is to ask, "How are you feeling now?", "What do you want from me now?", or "What can I do now so you'll quit being mad at me?"

Another common pitfall is the temptation to tell people what's going on in their heads. You can avoid this pitfall by first describing their specific behaviors and then asking what's going on instead of telling them: "Joe, when you came in to work this morning I said hello to you and you didn't respond. I then asked you if you had the report done, and you silently handed it to me. What are you feeling?" Or, you might even ask, "Are you mad at me?" We can observe behavior, and maybe we can make some pretty good guesses about what another person is feeling, but we do not really know what motivates someone, or what thinking/feeling is behind their behavior, unless we ask. The conclusions we draw about other people's behavior are often inaccurate. Even if our guesses are accurate, to tell people how they are feeling, or why they are behaving in a certain way, merely invites defensiveness. If we want to know what is motivating a person's behavior, it makes sense to *ask* the only person who knows for sure, rather than simply inform him of our conclusions.

All too frequently, people do not restrict their arguments to one issue at a time. I may raise an issue with you, and in response you raise a similar or different issue about me. Also, I may bring up four issues at once instead of coming to closure on any one. If a person responded to my confrontation about something she did by telling me about something *I* did, I would invite her to hold that issue until we finished discussing the original issue.

Rhetorical questions are another pitfall. People often ask questions that they don't really want answered and that are in fact substitutes for statements: (angrily) "Why did you tell Sam that I didn't want to do what he asked me to do?" In this case, I am not actually trying to find out *why* you did it; I don't really want to know. I do want you to know that I'm angry about what you did, and possibly that I don't want you to do anything like that again. It would be more effective if I would say, "Mary, I'm mad at you for telling Sam that I didn't want to do what he asked me to do." Even if I did want to know "why," a "why-type" question might not be effective because that kind of question tends to invite defensiveness. ("Why?" is often reminiscent of such Critical Parent questions as "Why didn't you clean your room?" or "Why did you wet the bed?" and therefore tends to stimulate the Adapted Child.) Questions about what, where and how are better than questions about why. A question like "What are the reasons that you're late?" is often more effective than one like "Why are you late?" The first type of question is more likely to bring up *facts* that will be useful in solving the problem, while the second is more likely to bring up *excuses* that retard solution of the problem.

In confrontation, "you" messages invite defensiveness. An alternative is to send repetitive "I" messages that invite people to understand what you are saying: "Joe, I really feel irritated when I sit at my desk and I wait for work that I have been promised. When I receive the work late, I end up being unable to get my own work out on time."

Often, people play games instead of confronting others effectively. Within organizations, it is common to find one person playing NIGYSOB while the other person cooperates with Kick Me. For example, a supervisor asks a supervisee to meet a certain deadline, knowing full well that the supervisee is notorious for missing deadlines. What are the reasons that a supervisor would discount history and set up the same supervisee to miss another deadline? A supervisor would do much better to either not expect certain deadlines to be met or to deal with the repetitive problem in a sounder way, as outlined previously. On the other hand, what are the reasons that a supervisee would agree to meet a deadline and then not do it? It would appear that the supervisee wants to get kicked, and the supervisor wants to "catch" the person instead of to solve the problem.

Evidence of the Karpman Drama Triangle is often seen in businesses and organizations. This is apparent in the game of Courtroom, which is outlined in the next chapter. In general, it is advisable to avoid the roles of Persecutor, Rescuer, or Victim.

Please remember that people often engage in games and avoid confrontation in an attempt to protect themselves. This is another example of an OK motivation behind a not-OK behavior, and it is one with which I certainly have sympathy. Some people feel that they have to Be Perfect, and believe that they are commiting a felony (not just a minor misdemeanor) when they make an error. Supervisors, for example, often believe that making an error is tantamount to proving that they are not masculine, or that they are lousy supervisors. Human beings make mistakes, and can learn from their errors. I suggest that people strive for excellence rather than for perfection. Confrontation that comes from Nurturing Parent, Adult, or Natural

Child does not invite people to feel vulnerable and defensive, and it avoids the Be Perfect syndrome.

What are some other ways I can help people avoid being defensive?

If I am willing to model non-defensive acceptance of confrontation, this gives others permission to do the same. This is especially true for supervisors who are models for their employees and parents who are models for their children.

How do I avoid being defensive when I am confronted?

When you are on the receiving end of anger, or of any disagreement or confrontation, it is effective to do the opposite of discounting; that is, to take your own thinking and feeling into consideration, take the other person's thinking and feeling into consideration, and make sure that you agree on what you are disagreeing about. A good technique for making sure you understand the other person, and for avoiding defensiveness, is reflective listening. Reflective listening involves checking your perceptions by paraphrasing what you have just heard ("I understand that you are worried and angry because the report isn't ready for distribution at the meeting") before you respond to the confrontation ("It isn't ready because the copying machine has been out of order. We expect to have the copies ready before the meeting begins"). Almost anyone can tell you what you just said to them, word for word, but unless their Adult is plugged in, they aren't really listening to you. When they listen reflectively, their psychic energy is in their Adult and will therefore not be in their Critical Parent or Adapted Child. This means that they will avoid defensiveness, and thereby improve communication. If an employee is criticized by a customer, it is quite easy for him to become defensive. For example: "Mr. Smith, we just received your shipment, and the printing left out an important heading. I am really upset because this means that we cannot put out an important mailing and will likely lose a great deal of business." Defensive response: "This is the first time we've done this, and I'm sure there must be some mistake. You probably left it out of the original." Reflective listening: "Mr. Jones, I can certainly understand why you're unhappy. To receive material that is not what you wanted, which will then put you in a position of missing your own timetable, is certainly cause to be upset." The employee may then wish to gather more information.

119

through reflective listening. If the criticism turns out to be valid, the employee rectifies the situation as best he can. If it is not valid, he invites the customer to look at the facts. It would then be advisable for him to explore alternatives with the customer, and to offer constructive suggestions.

How do I encourage others to confront effectively?

People who are not used to expressing anger need a great deal of encouragement to do so. As stated previously, when a person is willing to be angry with you, especially if he is willing to express his anger in a reasonable way, it is a real sign that he trusts you. He trusts that you will not leave him, fire him, be hurt in return, or be hostile in return. He trusts that you are strong enough to handle his anger and will not fall apart. Therefore, when you have encouraged people to level in a sensitive way, it is vitally important that you understand and respond to them instead of being defensive. Please be aware that people who are not used to showing anger are likely to do so from Rebellious Child or Critical Parent in the initial phases. How often I have seen executives get distressed when a TA training program invites leveling within their organization! Their subordinates start leveling, and the executives then tend to believe that they are losing the respect of those employees, rather than see this changed behavior as the positive sign it is: If the subordinates say it straight, they won't have to show it crooked and cost the organization hundreds, thousands, or millions of dollars through their passive-aggressive behaviors.

Chapter IX

HOW DO I APPLY TRANSACTIONAL ANALYSIS TO SUPERVISION?

The principles we've discussed so far are equally important to effective supervision. They work especially well in an "OK organization."

What's an OK organization?

An OK organization is a group or business that, by policy, takes into account the needs, wants and feelings of people—personnel, management, customers, constituents, students, faculty, patients, staff, stockholders, board of directors, inmates, the public, etc. The goals of the organization are clear, and its energies are expended toward accomplishing its purposes. It is aware of its place in, and its responsibilities to, the community, the environment, and whatever segment of the world is affected by its activities. It would, for example, avoid polluting the environment or engaging in unethical or discriminatory practices. Insofar as possible, an OK organization provides a healthy and comfortable environment for its members, physically and emotionally. It fosters cooperation rather than competition among its members. It is willing to learn about human behavior and motivation, and it uses this information to improve the quality of life and to increase consumer satisfaction rather than in an attempt to manipulate people. These attitudes serve to increase the "bottom line."

It sounds as if my organization is not OK. What can I do about this?

If your organization tends to be not OK, you have a number of options. You can work within it, protecting yourself so that *you* remain OK whether it is or not. You can encourage change in the organization, on a small scale or a large one. Or, you may decide that the best thing for you is to leave the organization. Only you can make the decision, and there are many factors to consider. One of them is your position within the organization. The farther up the hierarchy you are, the more impact your personal change can have on your organization. The president of a company, for example, can foster OK-ness throughout the organization. On the other hand, the newest worker on the assembly line can encourage changes from the bottom up, through OK dealings with his co-workers and his immediate supervisor. Committee chairmen, department and division heads, office supervisors, all can affect their immediate environments and those they supervise. Because the supervisor-supervisee relationship is so important in fostering an OK organization, this chapter will concentrate on effective supervision.

What are the essentials of supervision?

Supervision is the provision of guidance, feedback and structure in pursuit of agreed-upon objectives. Sound supervision is a process in which the supervisor and supervisee share ideas, information, and feelings on an authentic basis. It is therefore vitally important for the supervisor to create an atmosphere in which people are free to express their Natural Child wants, needs and feelings. The goal is to help the supervisee become as autonomous in accomplishing his responsibilities as his job description will permit, and to promote his job satisfaction. Transactionally speaking, the supervisor and supervisee are striving for OK, complementary transactions.

If you wish to improve your supervisory or managerial effectiveness, it's a good idea to examine your own personal background. Who are you? Presuming that you supervise from your Parent ego state, at least in part, there is an excellent chance that in your supervision you are imitating the way your parents parented you. For example, if they tended to be understanding in the midst of an error that you made, then it's likely that you will be understanding when a supervisee makes an error. You will probably resolve conflicts in a similar way, or be arbitrary in the resolution of conflicts, if that's how your parents handled similar situations. If your parents were generous in giving strokes—positive, conditional strokes for your performance as well as unconditional strokes just for being you—it's likely that you also stroke generously. You will tend to imitate the manner in which your parents confronted other people's shortcomings. Were they open to constructive criticism from you? If so, that increases the probability that you'll be open to constructive criticism from the people you supervise. If they asked for what they wanted, or were receptive to your asking for what you wanted, again you would have a tendency to model that behavior. In short, whether or not you agree with their methods, the important people in your childhood have probably had a great effect on the way you supervise today. Now, with your Adult, you can examine the parenting behaviors you learned as a child and decide which ones you want to keep. You can decide to turn off your

Critical Parent and think before you act. The better you know yourself, the more you are in control of the ineffective parts of your personality. Here's an exercise you can use to take a good look at yourself as a supervisor and decide what changes you want to make:

WHO ARE YOU AS A SUPERVISOR?

1. Were your parents basically nurturing or critical?
   What kinds of messages did you hear, and what was modeled, about:
   working?
   relaxing?
   stroking?
   being perfect?
   Do you convey the same messages to your supervisees?
   If your answers are not satisfactory to you, what will you do about it?

2. How did your parents resolve conflicts?
   Do you handle your own and your supervisees' conflicts in the same way?
   If your answers are not satisfactory to you, what will you do about it?

3. What kind of strokes do you give?
   Does it seem that you don't have time to do anything more than give directions or confront not-OK behavior?
   If your answers are not satisfactory to you, what will you do about it?

4. How do you confront the shortcomings of those you supervise?
   From what ego states do you confront?
   Do you do this in front of others?
   If your answers are unsatisfactory, what will you do about it?

5. Are you open to constructive criticism from supervisees and peers as well as from supervisors?
   If your answer is unsatisfactory, what will you do about it?

6. Do you ask for what you want, and do you expect others to do the same?

   If the answer to this is unsatisfactory, what will you do about it?

7. Do you handle your feelings effectively? (For example, what did you do the last time you were angry?)

   If you are not satisfied with the way you handled your feelings, what will you do the next time?

Who are you supervising? What are their Parent, Adult and Child ego states like? What are their needs, wants, feelings, thoughts and attitudes? How are they like you? How are you like them? You all have Natural Child needs, wants and feelings, and you all have the capacity for sound thinking. Their six ego states are probably quite similar to yours. There is no question that you all have the potential for OK-ness and not-OK-ness and that you will, from moment to moment, invite one another into OK-ness and not-OK-ness. All of you are likely to respond in OK ways as well as in not-OK ways. You are alike in that you all have inherent worth and dignity that must be respected. All of you can learn to keep your transactions OK.

What are the pitfalls of supervision?

Some pitfalls are the result of your own scripting and your own positions of OK-ness and not-OK-ness. You have made many childhood decisions that affect your present relationships—decisions concerning yourself, others (men, women, peers, subordinates, superiors), work, strokes, perfection, strength, etc. Some of these decisions may be impairing your effectiveness as a supervisor.

Another serious pitfall is emotional symbiosis, a subject to be discussed more fully in Chapter X. As a supervisor, you may have a tendency to seek and continue symbiotic relationships in which you and your subordinates have an unhealthy dependence upon each other. Without being aware of it, you may set up situations where one of you has a wish to parent and the other has a wish to be parented. One person does the thinking and takes care of the other by being nurturing or critical, while the responding person is either compliant or rebellious. In a symbiosis, people have a tendency to reverse positions but seldom relate Natural Child-to-Natural Child or Adult-to-Adult. Unfortunately, supervisors (and even presidents of companies) often exclude their Child ego states and function from Adult and Parent. Solutions to this problem will be discussed in the next chapter.

124

Organizations themselves are often symbiotic. The supervisors, from president on down, are in Parent and Adult, and the supervisees are in Adapted Child. With their supervisees, each individual is in Parent and Adult; with their own supervisors, they flip into Adapted Child. From the way these symbiotic organizations function, it's clear that the supervisor leaves his Natural Child on the coat-rack with his hat. The supervisor is viewed as someone needing no strokes and having no personal wants. On the other hand, the supervisee is stroked for not-OK behavior. He is not expected to think and be creative, nor is he expected to have legitimate wants which can be taken into consideration. Often, the supervisee extracts from the supervisor whatever energy and motivation is needed for getting things done. They are symbiotic in terms of psychic energy; the supervisee is dependent upon the supervisor for the motivation to do a creative job.

Another serious pitfall in supervision is the problem of *transference*. If I still have unresolved feelings toward my mother, my father, or other people who were important in my childhood, I tend to allow those feelings to distort my present relationships. As was stated earlier, *transference* means to transfer unfinished feelings from the past into the present. It can also be seen as an "as if" relationship: I see you *as if* you were somebody else (for example, a critical mother or father). The problem of transference is especially acute in a supervisory relationship. The supervisor can be in Adult, Nurturing Parent or Natural Child and nevertheless be viewed by the supervisee as being in Critical Parent. The response, from the supervisee's Adapted Child, is either compliance or rebellion. For example, Mrs. Smith, president of a large organization, asks Mr. Jones whether he has finished the budget yet. Mr. Jones' response is to feel guilty and inadequate and to stutter as he talks to her. Essentially he is in Compliant Child, seeing his dad confronting him about something he did, just as it happened in childhood. He re-experiences the same fear, guilt, and general sense of not-OK-ness, and this happens despite the fact that Mrs. Smith was merely making an Adult request for information. Mr. Green, on the other hand, responds to the same question by slamming the door and walking out in a very rebellious manner. Again, the same childhood feelings are re-lived, despite the fact that this situation is in no way similar to what Mr. Green's mom did to him.

Many other examples of transference occur within organizations.

How often have you seen a change in people's behavior when their boss enters the room? Some may quit thinking and almost stutter when they see him. Others may get suspicious and clam up. Many may abruptly turn off Natural Child behaviors. A few may start "showing off," acting in ways designed to please or impress the boss. In such instances, the boss is seen as if he were someone else, an individual from the employee's past with whom he has unfinished feelings. The boss is then responded to from Adapted Child. (These examples presume that the boss's behavior, past and present, doesn't warrant these responses.)

The boss may also indulge in transference transactions. He may, for example, have certain erroneous Parent beliefs about what subordinates are like or what women are like. He may therefore see a subordinate as being either compliant or rebellious when in fact she is not. He tends to respond to an Adult stimulus from the subordinate as if it were coming from Adapted Child; his response is from Critical Parent or Nurturing Parent. An example of this kind of transference occurs when Mrs. White, from Adult asks Mr. Smith for some information regarding a project he wanted done. Mr. Smith responds by telling her to calm down and not be so excited. In fact, Mrs. White was not excited and didn't need to be calmed down. She was simply wanting information. Given the same stimulus from Mrs. White, Mr. Smith could see her as being rebellious and therefore respond by being very abrupt with her. In either case, Mrs. White is likely to be puzzled by the inappropriate response.

Childhood experiences and modeling can create another supervisory problem: games. Parents model for their children how to play games, and children learn readily what roles to play in their own games with their parents. They become accustomed to playing the role of Persecutor, Victim, or Rescuer in the family games. Therefore, as a supervisor or supervisee, they will have a tendency to play the old, familiar role and to invite others to play complementary roles. Mr. Jones, for example, habitually fails to give his subordinates adequate information about the tasks he assigns to them. His subordinates will try to do the job, guessing at what he wants because they know it's not OK to ask for clarification (Kick Me-Victim). Mr. Jones later finds fault with the quality of their work (NIGYSOB-Persecutor). They all end up with bad feelings of resentment and mistrust (the payoff).

Supervisors often initiate games of NIGYSOB when they discount information they have about their subordinates. For example, a supervisor may ask a subordinate to complete a task by a certain deadline, even though she knows full well that he frequently misses deadlines. Rather than dealing effectively with this continuing problem, she initiates a game of NIGYSOB by asking the subordinate to agree to do something and discounting the fact that he often breaks such contracts. When the subordinate agrees to take on the task, with full awareness of his difficulties in meeting contracts, he sets up a complementary game of Kick Me. Sure enough, when the deadline arrives and the task is not completed, the supervisor gets angry, and the subordinate feels guilty and sometimes put-upon. Both supervisors and supervisees can set up games of NIGYSOB by discounting early signs that things are going wrong. They could stop something before it becomes a full-blown problem, but instead they wait until the misdemeanor becomes a felony. Then they say the equivalent of "gotcha!"

The general comments made earlier concerning the antitheses to transference and games certainly apply in the area of supervision. Likewise, the concepts of Potency, Permission and Protection are applicable. A supervisor who is potent is a person who is self-confident and appropriately assertive. His Potency is demonstrated by consistent modeling of effective work; he is a person who practices what he expects of others. A supervisor can give Permission through verbal messages (It's OK to . . ."), but the most potent permission is given where he models the behavior he expects of others. For example, a supervisor who is willing to accept confrontation invites his supervisees to receive and benefit from confrontation instead of becoming defensive when confronted. A supervisor who expects his crew to be budget-conscious gives them permission to be budget-conscious when he demonstrates frugality himself. A common complaint of subordinates is that they are on tight budgets while their boss makes exotic expenditures. People receive undesirable permissions just as easily as they respond to the modeling of positive behaviors. For example, when a supervisor complains to others about his boss, he is giving permission to his subordinates to take their complaints about him to third parties instead of to him.

A supervisor provides Protection in a number of ways. For example, it is comforting for supervisees to know that their supervisor is available to them, especially when a problem arises, and that he stands by his agreements. "Protection" does not imply that the supervisor shields his supervisees from the results of their actions. Rather, it means that the supervisees can count on him to act in a straightforward and impartial manner. When a customer or other employee complains about one of his subordinates, the effective supervisor remains neutral and keeps the focus on solution of the problem. Subordinates feel protected when they realize that a supervisor will be fair and square, even if this means that he will confront and disagree with them. The three P's lead to effective communication and effective supervision.

Structure and *strokes* are important elements of effective supervision. They are the bases for encouraging behavioral changes and accurate implementation of new programs. The next several pages will focus on practical ways of meeting people's Natural Child need for structure and on several types of structure that are required for sound supervision. There are necessary structures for supervisory sessions, for hiring, for firing, for decision-making, for assumption of responsibility, and so on. When elements such as *who, when, how, where* and *what* are clearly defined and consistently implemented, the supervisee finds his job more comfortable. His need to test, to see whether the supervisor means what he says, is diminished when appropriate structure is provided.

What about the supervisory conference?

The coming-together of the supervisor and supervisee to deal with ongoing issues of the organization is referred to as the "supervisory conference." This meeting is best scheduled at the same time each week, or semi-monthly. I hasten to say that if there is no sound purpose for a particular meeting, it need not take place; nevertheless, the meetings should be scheduled at regular intervals and cancelled only by mutual consent. The positive effect on a person's Child is that he can plan for and depend on that exclusive time with you; it tells him that he is important to you. This is not to say that there isn't a place for the informal chat or the phone call, which are often necessities. Some supervisors have an open-door policy, which has its assets and the obvious liability of infringement upon the supervisor's time.

The conference is a time that should be uninterrupted by phone calls or letter-opening. It is a time when you can sit face to face, without a desk hiding either of you. It is a time when it's OK to sip coffee, to feel relaxed and comfortable. In general, it is vital to create a physical and emotional atmosphere in which a person feels free to share feelings and thoughts, and in which he is convinced that he will be heard and responded to appropriately.

What's the difference between individual and group sessions?

Group supervision can be extremely efficient and effective. It is advantageous when there are issues of concern common to all. Group supervision is also helpful when the focus is to create a team atmosphere. It is often a time-saver. As does individual supervision, group supervision provides opportunities for stroking the Child. A stroke given in front of a group can be especially gratifying, and there are more sources of strokes. Group supervision offers an opportunity to hear what others are doing and stroke them; you can also share your own ideas and receive strokes for them.

Confrontation is best done on an individual basis. A person is more likely to receive constructive criticism from his Adult when he is not confronted in front of his peers. Individual supervision is also advantageous when you are working with an individual's specific problems. Occasionally, for an individual to have "his time" with his supervisor is very valuable in meeting his Child needs for stroking and recognition.

What should be covered in a supervisory conference?

Content should be agreed upon, at least in part, at the previous conference. The agenda will often include certain standard issues that require weekly discussion: the budget, sales, production, etc. Another important conference issue will be the natural reporting on results of the previous conference. This provides for *accountability;* when a directive is given or a decision is made, it is automatically built into the agenda for the following conference. Direct observation is another valuable way of getting content for a conference. For example, I might like to see how each of my salespeople deals with a customer, or observe the way the receptionists answer the phone, so that I can help them to increase their effectiveness or stroke them for specific things they are doing exceptionally well. It goes without saying that I will not eavesdrop, sneak up on these people, or surprise them; observation requires the supervisee's advance agreement. Another valuable tool for planning conference content is a special file folder with the supervisor or supervisee's name on it. As issues or questions arise, a simple note can be dropped into that file, so that both supervisor and supervisee can remember important issues they might otherwise forget to bring up. These notes can then be used in preparation for the conference.

Preparation for the supervisory conference is highly important. It may take no more than five or ten minutes to outline what you're wanting to deal with and accomplish during the session. It is advisable that both supervisor and supervisee do this. The content of the conference is enhanced by role-playing and modeling; that is, if a supervisee is to set limits or confront someone, he may need to hear you do it, or to rehearse this action with you while you play the role of either the confronter or the confrontee. These techniques can be valuable in helping the supervisee prepare to deal with ticklish problems. After seeing your demonstration, or rehearsing with you, he is better prepared to handle the problem competently and comfortably.

Please keep this fact in mind: *Supervisors don't need to know all the answers.* If you don't know the answer, say so.

I believe it is vitally important to include "leveling time" in the agenda for each supervisory conference. I have found that subordinates are much more willing to level with their supervisor, both positively and negatively, if there is a structure for it. Supervisors also benefit from a structure for leveling. It increases their willingness to confront and solve problems instead of burying their heads in the sand, and it ensures opportunities for them to give positive strokes.

The contract for leveling time is that the supervisor and supervisee will share authentic feelings in a constructive way. For example, one may feel like giving positive strokes for something the other did since their last meeting, or for effective work in general. One may have a positive unconditional stroke for the other. One may want to let the other know that he has negative feelings about certain of the other's behaviors and what he would like the other to do about it. One may have constructive feedback or constructive criticism for the other. The agreement is that positive strokes and confrontation will be heard and acknowledged, that there will be no *unconditional* negative strokes, and that confrontation will focus on the desired result. In other words, instead of saying, "Don't do that," the confronter says, "I'd like you to do this instead."

As a consultant, I invite organizations to make it clear that leveling is expected and valued. Leveling cannot be initiated by directive alone, however. Unless a boss models acceptance of constructive criticism and shows that he can deal effectively with other people's expressions of negative feelings, it is unlikely that his subordinates will be willing to level with him. I invite you, as a supervisor, to consider letting your subordinates know that their leveling ability will be one factor taken into consideration for promotion. Poeple who can learn to level in a sensitive and caring way make the best kinds of supervisors.

Who should decide what?

Be prepared to accept others' decisions if you have given them the responsibility for making those decisions. If you are asking people for their ideas, but wish to retain the privilege of making the decision yourself, then say so. For example, "I have a decision to make, and I'd like to know what you think about it before I decide." It's OK to change decisions when you have new information. It's important not to confuse consistency with rigidity. In decision-making, *consistency* is taking a position based upon logical thinking- and sticking with it. *Flexibility* is the willingness to change the original decision, based upon new information. *Inconsistency* is changing the decision without sound reason, based upon whim or feeling, while *rigidity* is taking a position and sticking to it, even though there are sound reasons for changing it.

Effective supervision encourages people to think and to make their own decisions within the scope of their responsibilities. If it is my responsibility to make a decision and I want you to make it for me, it behooves you to decline. That's an invitation to Rescue, and if you accept it you're very likely to end up as a Victim. (For instance, if you tell me how to handle something and the method doesn't work, you can then feel like a failure. Or I can switch to Persecutor and blame you for the failure.) If people aren't using the information they have for making a decision, point that out to them. If they need information in order to make a decision, give it to them. When a supervisee has a disagreement with organizational policy, or with a directive of the supervisor, that disagreement should be handled directly with the supervisor instead of with others (as in, "It's the boss's idea, and I don't agree with it"). This is inappropriate and diminishes the person's potency. If you discuss it with the boss and still don't get satisfaction, then you can resolve to accept the decision without feeling a need to air the disagreement publicly.

What is the supervisor's role in conflicts between his subordinates?

It is important for a supervisor to avoid assuming the role of judge and jury when people come to him with complaints about a third party, or when a "plaintiff" and "defendant" appear in his office. Whenever possible, it is of great value for the boss to encourage a complainant to deal directly with the person with whom he is in conflict. This may be facilitated by discussion about how that could be done, or by a role-playing rehearsal. Sometimes the complainant will not go to the appropriate party, and in those instances a boss must handle the complaint by staying objective and neutral and perhaps by inviting a three-way conference.

In any three-way conference when one person is unhappy about someone else's actions, it is important to avoid being a Rescuer or a Persecutor. It is quite easy to get into a game of Courtroom in this kind of situation. To avoid Courtroom, it is advisable for the boss to ask the people to talk to each other instead of telling him about their complaints. He would intervene only to keep the discussion focused on the issue, on resolution of the conflict, and on making an appropriate contract. In some cases it is to everyone's advantage for the boss to insist that they resolve the conflict in a way that's mutually beneficial and beneficial for the organization.

Is it ever OK to go over someone's head?

Needless to say, going over someone's head is very risky business, yet it is a common problem within organizations. When you are in conflict, I strongly advise that you do your best to resolve the conflict with the person in question. This may require confrontation and some form of escalation over a period of time, but it is almost always preferable to going over someone's head. If you decide that you must take such action, first be certain that you are and have been straight with your supervisor. One intermediate step is to talk to one of your boss's peers about the difficulty, to seek his counsel and perhaps his intervention. If this isn't satisfactory, then invite your supervisor to go with you to get some objective feedback from the boss. Notice that you want to completely avoid the business of "I'm going to tell on you." If the supervisor refuses to accompany you, indicate that you intend to go by yourself and let him know what you're planning to say. In some cases a supervisor may be very much opposed to your going to his boss, and I urge you not to take any such action unless you are willing to risk his rejection.

How can I facilitate the assumption of new roles or responsibilities?

The often-quoted Peter Principle[1] is an underlying issue when one talks about new responsibilities: Will the person now reach his level of incompetence? How can you tell whether a person is ready to handle a new project, a different role, or a promotion? How can you help him become ready?

The fact that I can sell doesn't necessarily mean that I can supervise other salespeople effectively. Although this concept is widely understood, it is often discounted. Also, the fact that I am capable of being an adequate regional manager doesn't necessarily mean that I want all the hassles that come along with that job. Maybe my Child is comfortable with the level of responsibility I have right now and would rebel at the sacrifices this promotion would entail, making it difficult for me to work up to my capacity. But what will happen if I turn down this opportunity for advancement? People often take on jobs from an Adapted Child position. They may believe that they have no option, that if they don't take the job you want them to have, they'll be fired. They may take the job to please you, or to please their imaginary audience. They may believe that others "think you're a loser" if you don't want to be elevated in responsibility and/or status. Thus, from an adapted position, they may assume new responsibilities they'd really rather not have.

When you give a person a new responsibility, it is important to make sure that he accepts the responsibility because it holds some attraction for his Child and his Adult thinks it makes sense for him. Questions like "What's in it for you to take this job?" "Do you really *want* the job?" "What are your reasons for wanting this new responsibility?" "Does it make sense for you?" can help both of you to determine his investment in the proposed change.

It is also important to make sure that the person will have what he needs to do the job. Some organizations create serious problems by giving a person responsibility and failing to give him the authority to go along with it. This often occurs when a boss is uncomfortable with the delegation of authority. It puts the subordinate in a difficult situation: Although he is responsible, he is not in charge. He must go to his supervisor for even mundane decisions, and his effectiveness is severely impaired. Because his subordinates are aware that he has

133

little real power, they tend to go over his head to his boss, who doesn't provide the support that he needs. This kind of unfortunate situation can be avoided by matching responsibility with authority. If you don't think a person deserves the authority that goes with a certain job, it would be best not to give him that responsibility. One helpful way of delegating authority is to set up guidelines limiting the kinds of decisions a subordinate can make but allowing him a degree of autonomy commensurate with his responsibilities. For example, he can make decisions for expenditures up to a certain limit, or within a given budget. He has the authority to do X but not Y. The better spelled-out these guidelines are, the easier it is for the person to function.

How do I decide who to hire?

Several of the principles that are useful in facilitating an employee's assumption of new roles and responsibilities are equally important in the selection of new employees. First, it is important to make sure that the person *wants* the job and that it makes sense for him to have the job. Then, is is well to determine whether the applicant has adequate "people skills" in addition to the technical skills needed for the job, and whether his predominant ego states are compatible with the requirements of the position.

I have found that personnel staff tend to hire employees whose predominant ego states are complimentary to their own. Critical Parent tends to hire Compliant Child, the Compliant Child ego state tends to hire other Compliant Children or Nurturing Parents, the Nurturing Parent ego state tends to hire Compliant Children, the Adult tends to hire Adults, and so on. People with a healthy mix of Nurturing Parent, Adult, and Natural Child tend to hire individuals who also operate in those effective ego states. It would make more sense, however, to hire people on the basis of whether their predominant ego states fit the job. People who are high in Nurturing Parent, Adult, and Natural Child function very well in a wide variety of positions; however, this type of person is not necessarily well suited to every job. For example, an employee who is high in Compliant Child and low in Adult may be more content in a position involving menial or repetitive tasks and therefore may be a better choice for that job. It is important to identify the primary ego state or states that the job requires and then determine during the interview (with your Little Professor as well as with your Adult) whether the applicant ranks

134

high in the necessary ego states. Some simple questions added to the interview can elicit this kind of information, particularly if the interviewer remembers to pay attention to non-verbal clues as well as to the answers.

Questions like these are helpful in eliciting information about an applicant's Child ego state:

> What do you do in your spare time?
>
> Why do you want this job?
>
> At work, is there a time when joking and having fun is OK? Please explain.

To test the security of the person's Child, you might ask, "What would you like to tell me about yourself?" or "What do you have to offer us?" or "What do you see as your assets or limitations?" When he doesn't know the answer to one of your questions, does he try to fake it? Or does he admit that he doesn't know? Does he ask questions? Is he interviewing you? Does he make good eye contact? Positive answers to several of these questions indicate that his Child takes an "I'm OK" position.

To gain information about his Adult ego state, ask questions pertaining to situations he will be likely to encounter on the job. This will tell you how well he thinks on his feet. Watch out for "cop-out answers." Does he understand well? If he doesn't understand, is he willing to ask for clarification? Does he conceptualize well? Does he communicate well? Does he ask intelligent questions?

To assess his Parent ego state, you can ask questions regarding his value systems, attitudes, et cetera. What are his attitudes about work, hours, pay, having fun, dress, language? Does he listen well? To assess his Nurturing Parent, you can ask questions about work situations that would require an understanding and caring response. For example, "What would you say to a customer who was complaining about X?"

What else is important to look for?

How does the applicant present herself in general? Is she assertive? Does she initiate topics? Does she simply follow your lead? What is indicated by her grooming and the clothing she has chosen to wear to the interview? What about the volume and tone of her voice?

How much does the applicant discount? When you ask a question, does she answer it? Or does she answer a different question? Is she vague? Is she alert? Does she interrupt? How does she handle being interrupted by you?

Make sure that the person's Child wants the job and that her Adult understands the responsibilities, time commitment, lines of authority, and compensation. This is best done by having a written job description available that she can look over and agree to before she accepts the job. Charts showing lines of authority and manuals outlining policies and procedures are helpful in the hiring process. Once she's on the job they become almost mandatory as important forms of structure.

What about references?

In general, it is fair to say that applicants give as references the names of people they think will give them a good rating. When I contact references I often ask them to be objective about the applicant. Sometimes, I tend to put them on the spot by asking such questions as, "If you were in my shoes, would you hire her?" "Is she the kind of person you would want to have working for a member of your family?" "What are her strengths and limitations?" These kinds of questions will often elicit a more complete, sincere response than you might otherwise get.

What are the special needs of people with new jobs?

It is important to make support available to people who are learning new jobs or shouldering new responsibilities. A sink-or-swim attitude can invite potentially capable individuals to flounder. It is common for people to need extra strokes from their supervisors during these times.

When a person is given a new responsibility, often he would like your Nurturing Parent to be understanding of his Child fears and insecurities. At the same time, you can give Adult information which will also be very supportive to his Child. Make sure the person knows the "how-to's" and be sure to model these. Also, be sure to follow up after giving directives on a new way of doing something. Great amounts of money are spent in making sure that people know "how to," and then the ball is dropped because their supervisors don't use the supervisory conference to determine whether the new methods are being implemented effectively. It is advisable to build into the agenda a discussion of the new system or new ideas and be prepared to discuss this periodically.

136

Is there any "good" way to fire somebody?

The principles discussed in Chapter VIII concerning confrontation and escalation apply here. The effective supervisor rarely has to fire anybody. She simply structures the situation so that the *employee* decides whether he will continue his employment and indicates his decision by his actions.

What about strokes on the job?

The general concepts we've discussed concerning positive and negative strokes are applicable in supervision. Some supervisors and supervisees seem to want, ask for, and/or give only negative strokes. Remember, if your Child needs for stroking are met by negative strokes, you will not feel the need for positive strokes as strongly. Conversely, if you change the negative stroke economy to a positive one, the need for negative strokes and the playing of games to get them will be diminished. Some supervisors and supervisees stroke only for performance and give no unconditional strokes. People usually resent this because it appears that they always have to "do something" to get acceptance. Some supervisors and supervisees won't accept positive strokes; in fact, this is quite common. If such people are presented with positive strokes, they will discount them either overtly or in their heads. Another common problem is that supervisees think that the boss doesn't need strokes, and the boss often agrees. She therefore goes around stroke-hungry. On the other hand, a supervisor may tend to see supervisees only to give a directive or to give negative strokes about something that was not done or done inappropriately. Once more, this often has to do with childhood programming and the ways in which people learn about strokes. Many stroking problems will be solved by changes in the supervisor's stroking patterns; some will not, because they are so deeply ingrained in the script of the supervisee.

Some people value certain kinds of strokes more highly than others, or find them easier to accept. For example, one supervisee may not accept a stroke about her appearance but may value highly a stroke for her intelligence. Another may not assimilate verbal strokes well but may be deeply affected by a friendly touch on the shoulder. The capable and caring supervisor remembers the importance of different strokes for different folks and looks for opportunities to give supervisees the kinds of positive strokes they prefer.

It is difficult to give nourishing, authentic-feeling strokes when you yourself are stroke-hungry. I suggest that you increase your supply of incoming strokes by making contracts for stroking with supervisees, peers, and supervisors: "Is it OK with you if occasionally I brag to you and ask you for compliments for what I've done? I'm willing to do the same for you." It is also a good idea to find someone within the organization with whom you can develop a trusting relationship. That person will not only serve as a source of stroking for you, he will also be a sounding-board when you are mulling over a problem or resolving a conflict with someone. Choose someone who has the strength to be objective. All too often, people choose the brightest person in the organization; that is, someone who will agree with them. Unfortunately, such people often have the same axes to grind as you do and will not really be helpful; the two of you may well end up playing "Ain't It Awful" or "If It Weren't for Them."

In summary, an effective supervisor gives three kinds of strokes: positive conditional strokes, negative conditional strokes when appropriate, and positive unconditional strokes. She does not give negative unconditional strokes. Her guideline is: "I stroke you for what you do, and I stroke you for being you." These two forms of positive strokes—conditional (for what you do) and unconditional (for being you)—are very healing, soothing, and energizing. They provide the charge that makes people's batteries run. Giving constructive negative strokes for what people do is also an important ingredient for real caring. You can keep your negative conditional strokes constructive by remembering to: (a) stroke from Nurturing Parent, Adult, and Natural Child; (b) tell the person how you feel about what he's doing, and ask for what you want instead; and (c) use do's instead of don'ts. Finally, your positive strokes will have more impact if you tailor them to the recipient—different strokes for different folks!

How can I increase the effectiveness of my department meeting or board meeting?

The guidelines I am about to present can help any group to function well, whether it is an ongoing group or a one-shot meeting. Many also apply to creating effective special events. Following these guidelines will eliminate boring meetings. It will also eliminate the practice of having meetings for meetings' sake, with no purpose in mind.

In general, a successful meeting will include three processes: *planning, decision-making,* and *assumption of responsibility.* A meeting that does not include at least two of these processes tends to be unsuccessful. If none of these three processes is to be included, there is no reason to hold a meeting —unless the purpose of the meeting is simply to provide structure for interpersonal communication in which positive stroking takes place.

One guideline for a successful meeting is to have *clear objectives* for that get-together. It is helpful to have more than one person, and perhaps several people, involved in determining the objectives of a meeting. This helps to increase the clarity of the objectives and the interest of the participants. It is well to state the objectives at the beginning of the meeting, so that the content of the meeting will relate to those objectives whether or not a formal agenda is followed.

Who plans the meeting agenda? A general rule is that the more participants are involved in the planning process, the better the meeting. I have seen many meetings fall on their faces because the department head did all the planning. Often agendas can be planned in advance by having participants communicate (in writing, by phone, or face-to-face), what they want to deal with at the meeting. It is also effective to devote time at the end of each meeting for planning the next meeting. When agendas are prepared in advance, participants have adequate time for preparation. It is well to distribute agendas prior to the meeting. When you plan or contribute to an agenda, make sure that there are opportunities for the three vital processes: *making decisions, assuming responsibility,* and *planning.* Many meetings are flops because they involve nothing more than sitting and listening to reports, with no opportunity to make contributions. Because the participants' brains are not being picked, they do not feel invested in the proceedings and may consider the meeting to be a waste of their valuable time. This is often the case when most of the important decisions have been made before the meeting. All too frequently, decisions are made by one person when it would be better to involve others. (The specifics of decision-making were discussed earlier in this chapter.) The more people responsible for active participation in a meeting, the better the chances are that the meeting will go well. If the only person who has anything to do at the meeting is the chairperson, others feel less involved.

When decisions are made during a meeting, it is valuable to also determine who will assume responsibility for follow-up or carrying out of the decisions. There are many reasons that it is well to include assumption of responsibility with the making of decisions. In a meeting, participants have the opportunity to contract for responsibilities that interest them or that are a logical part of their jobs. Not only does this often eliminate the necessity for *assigning* responsibilities, it also offers opportunity for stroking the person who is willing to take them on and helps to ensure that they will be carried out effectively.

Another important meeting process is *interpersonal communication.* Create an atmosphere that invites people to express their points of view, pro or con. This can be accomplished by stating that it is desirable for them to share their opinions with the group —and, more important, by lending an ear to those who make comments and stroking them for doing so. It is not necessary for all communication to take place through the chair. Informal discussion among members, in a fashion that promotes the purpose of the meeting, is beneficial. People really enjoy talking to one another, and relaxed or enthusiastic discussion often brings up creative material from the Natural Child ego states of the participants. Informal discussion can be especially valuable in meetings where sensitive leveling is important. (Please remember, however, that leveling sessions must be contracted for in advance and that issues involving the shortcomings of individuals are best handled on a one-to-one basis.) Meetings are important sources of strokes, yet many meetings are structured in ways that diminish opportunities for exchange of positive strokes among the participants. If stroking does not occur spontaneously or in response to modeling, it would be well to set up a specific structure for stroking. For example, a break may be scheduled in which participants are free to chat informally during the meeting, or a "stroking time" may be designated during which members are invited to express their approval or appreciation of each other's contributions.

Appropriate *structure* enhances a meeting. As you will remember, structure is a method for formalizing, dividing, and sharing responsibility, as well as for defining policies and procedures, and it is important that the agenda be structured to promote the process outlined in this section. Meetings do best when they start on time and last no longer than 1½ to 2 hours. Responsibilities can be structured: chairperson, committee chairpeople, ad hoc committee chairpeople, et cetera. Sometimes it is helpful to provide the structure of having a different person chair each meeting.

When people are actively involved in a meeting, they develop *esprit de corps,* a sense of oneness with the group. This feeling is not

140

only gratifying to individual participants, it also enhances the effectiveness of the group. These guidelines have suggested various ways of getting people involved, formally and informally, in the planning and processes of the meeting. *Involvement is the key to a successful meeting.*

How do I start implementing these ideas?

One way to start is to make clear contracts with your supervisor and/or supervisees. A contract, as stated earlier, is an agreement for mutual benefit. If you have been functioning in a certain way and are now planning to change your behavior, it is important that you share your plan with the people who will be affected by it. Sharing this information, including your reasons for the change, will make it more likely that your changed behavior will receive a positive response. For example, if you have not been asking for what you wanted, and you are now planning to ask, explain that and give your reasons. The mutuality of the supervisory conference necessitates agreement that it is a two-way process. This means that both people are responsible for preparing an agenda, for making decisions, and for assuming responsibility. It is also sound to contract for "no discounting." This means that you will be willing to accept confrontation from Nurturing Parent, Adult, or Natural Child, as well as to confront from the same ego states.

It is important for you to model asking for what you want and to make it clear that you expect others to do the same. Perhaps it goes without saying that it is vitally important to stick by commitments and let others know that you expect them to do so as well. Whenever possible, changes in commitments must be negotiated for and agreed upon. For example, if I've agreed to meet with you at a certain time and an important customer wants to meet with me at the same time, I must inform the customer that I will get back to him and then negotiate with you for a time change. If it is not feasible to put off possible conflicts in that way, then in my initial agreement to meet with you our contract will include an agreement that our appointment can be postponed if there is an urgent reason to do so, a matter of business necessity. Whenever a person agrees to do something, the agreement constitutes a contract, and that person is held accountable. It is important to confront the breach of any contract and to acknowledge responsibility for any that you breach, both from your Adult. If everybody in an organization can be counted upon to do what they say they will do, this is a major step in making an organization OK.

141

Chapter X

WHAT ABOUT MY PERSONAL LIFE?

How can I apply this material to my close relationships?

Whenever people talk about relationships, they also talk about intimacy. When Berne described the six ways of structuring time, he expressed his belief that people spend very little time in a state of true intimacy. I do not agree that the experience of intimacy is rare; rather, I believe that intimacy is experienced daily by many people. It is shared between members of the same sex as well as between members of the opposite sex. It is experienced between parent and child, between co-workers, among relatives and friends, and sometimes with chance acquaintances. As I see it, intimacy is simply the authentic sharing of feelings, especially the four *natural* feelings: anger, sadness, fear, and warmth. It is also the open expression of a person's needs and wants, and the appropriate responses of others. We have already noted that intimacy involves Natural Child-to-Natural Child transactions. It also involves transactions between Nurturing Parent and Natural Child.

Trust is essential if people are to be intimate. For example, it takes real trust to be willing to express anger to people who are important to you. If I am going to share my angry feelings with you, I must trust that you will not leave or reject me. I must trust that you are secure enough to avoid feeling rejected as a person if I express my anger about what you are doing.

Richard Underhill* has said, "If you can't say 'no' and mean it, you can't say 'yes' and mean it." One way of saying "no" is to say "yes" and then not do what you have agreed to do. Disagreeing in a straight and sensitive way is an expression of intimacy.

In business, intimacy is often achieved when people level with each other, when they let each other know where they stand. In intimacy, people can disagree without putting each other down. When people are leveling with each other in a sensitive way, they can give and accept confrontation more easily. Intimacy on the job also takes the form of giving positive strokes to people for what they do, as well as just for being themselves. In a work situation, people's intimacy creates an environment where people feel accepted and respected

*Richard Underhill, Ph.D.,is an educator and consultant in Richmond, Virginia, and a Special Fields Teaching Member of the ITAA.

and therefore enjoy their work. When people do not level with each other at work, the results can be disastrous: employees do not enjoy their work; they do not express what they think and feel; they simply hurt, quietly. (If they do express their thoughts and feelings, they usually don't do so with anyone who might be able to correct the situation. Instead, they talk to the person who is most likely to agree with them.) Often employees end up getting fired, still without having developed real awareness of what they were doing that needed changing.

When I care about people, I am willing to share my feelings about what they are doing and ask for what I want from them instead. When people are intimate with one another, they often have a sense of "oneness" and an energy flow between them that leads to great pleasure and a sense of well-being. As with any form of intimacy, leveling with others in a sensitive way requires that I see people as possessing inherent worth and dignity. Because I believe this, I want to deal with others in a caring, understanding and responsive manner.

Although I disagree that intimacy is "rare," I do agree that it is an elusive state. Many investigators have explored the reasons for this. Blanck and Blanck,[27] who are well known in the psychoanalytic school of thought, have made reference to various types of *fears* as one basis for people's difficulties in life and, to my way of thinking, as a key reason for avoiding intimacy with one another. These fears arise in sequence during a child's early development. If the child's needs and wants are met during each stage of development, so that each developmental fear is resolved as it comes up, the child will become a complete, healthy human being who is not afraid to share intimacy with others. If some of these fears are left unresolved, they become blocks to intimacy in adulthood. Some people fear that they will be annihilated; some fear that they will be abandoned, or rejected. These deep-seated fears can be resolved in adulthood; it is not too late to fill in the developmental steps that were skipped in childhood.

Often, people will make reference to "having been intimate at one time" and ending up as a loser. It is significant that, when these people are questioned about their "losing" relationships, there is seldom much evidence that they were consistently open with their mates, friends, or employees. Usually, it becomes clear that they were ultimately rejected because of *lack* of intimacy. If you are having trouble in your personal relationships, I invite you to question the sources of your fears and examine your past relationships. Were you rejected because you were open with the other person, or because you were not open enough? Was some childhood experience responsible for your reluctance to share intimacy with that person? I believe that fear is a primary reason for people's difficulty in achieving intimacy. Insensitivity is another reason, one that also stems from failure to complete childhood developmental tasks. It is difficult to respond appropriately to the needs and wants of others when you experience yourself as needy and unfulfilled. If that is the case, you will tend to compete for what is available rather than to share freely. Others will sense this attitude, and perhaps will decide not to be with you. If you are competing for strokes that are freely available, you are inviting the kinds of psychological games that destroy relationships.

Dr. Stephen Karpman has pointed out a specific fear that blocks intimacy: people are afraid that if they really get close to another person, that person will make them change their whole way of life as the price of closeness.[28] That idea certainly rang true to me! At one time, I was afraid to get really close to another person because I was afraid I would then lose my individuality, that I would have to give up my friends, that I wouldn't be able to do some of the things I always wanted to do. Now I know that, in truly intimate relationships, there is a give-and-take process that allows both parties to meet their needs and wants. Most issues can be handled by negotiation and compromise; rarely is it necessary to make an actual sacrifice.

Karpman develops his thesis by saying that, because of the fear of having to change one's whole way of life, a person enters a Loser's Loop; that is, he or she develops certain attitudes that keep people at a distance. There are any number of Loser's Loops, but most are a variation of two basic types: the CASE Loop and the ERA Loop. A person who blocks intimacy with the CASE loop does so by being Condescending, Abrupt, Secretive, and Evasive. Once more, Karpman's ideas had a familiar ring to me. Whenever I have been condescending, abrupt, secretive, or evasive, I have ended up alone. People who use the ERA Loop are Eager, Relentless and Annoying. This behavior usually inspires the use of the CASE loop by others, in self-defense.

There are thousands of ways in which people invite distance and elude intimacy. For example, people create distance when they are in Critical Parent, Rebellious Child, or Compliant Child. They create distance when they give more negative strokes than positive ones. When they get into "driver behavior"[29] (Hurry Up, Be Perfect, Be Strong, Try Hard, Please Me) they create distance between themselves and others. When people expect others to *know* (through mind-reading) how they feel and what they want, when they discount other people, allow others to discount them, or fail to express their thoughts and feelings, they create distance and avoid intimacy.

The programs for intimacy as well as for distance, for joy as well as for misery, are largely decided upon in childhood. The decisions we make and the methods we choose for carrying them out are influenced greatly by what we observe in our own families. As we watch our mothers and fathers, we learn how a man relates to a woman and a woman relates to a man. We note which feelings are acceptable, which are unacceptable, what methods may not be used, and so on. From these observations, we decide how to get along in our family — and in the world. We decide whether we want our future relationships to be like the one our parents have modeled. Whether or not we like their relationship, however, we will tend to develop the same kind for ourselves. Unfortunately, we often create very similar relationships in our own marriages, even though we may have resolved that "this will never happen to me." We may choose to marry someone who seems to have characteristics the opposite of those our mother or father had; to our dismay, that person often turns out to be more like Mom or Dad than we would like to admit even to ourselves. Often we marry someone who is very much like the mother or father who never accepted us. We can then continue the same struggle for acceptance throughout our lives.

The same phenomenon takes place within organizations. Essentially, organizations —and sometimes departments within organizations —are "families." These "families" have "parents." They also have "children" who watch the parent or parents and, based on these observations, make a variety of decisions about what's OK and what's not OK, how close they can get, and how much distance they will create. Modeling by supervisors is the major factor determining whether leveling will ever take place within an organization. When supervisors model openness, their employees will often be more open.

Hogie Wyckoff[30] has done an excellent job in pointing out how our society contributes to the lack of intimacy we experience in our country. (This is not to say that other cultures do not suffer from the same difficulty; they do, but the causes may differ.) When she talks about "sexist scripting," she makes the point that children, in the books they read, the television they watch, the advertising they are exposed to, are taught that men are not supposed to show feelings and women are not supposed to think. If intimacy involves Natural Child-Natural Child or Nurturing Parent-Natural Child transactions, then how will this ever be attained if men are not supposed to feel? (Of course, certain feelings are culturally unacceptable for women, too—especially anger.) If problem-solving and constructive planning are done with Adult-Adult transactions, how can this ever be accomplished if women aren't supposed to think? In a society that promotes these ideas, it's no wonder there is an ever-increasing divorce rate.

Is it unrealistic to want intimacy?

Despite the fact that so many people consider intimacy to be unattainable, I strongly believe that it *is* attainable and that it is experienced by many people, regularly. I will be intimate, however, only after I decide that I really like myself. Until I make this decision, I am not willing to truly like and care about somebody else and do not have the energy for building intimate relationships. Only after I decide that everybody is OK am I willing to look at my own limitations, instead of believing that I am always right and you are always wrong, or vice versa. When my basic position is "I'm OK, you're OK," I will not need to spend my time "trying" to change you; instead, I will focus on how *I* can be more effective in my interactions with you, and thereby invite you to change. I may simply decide to accept you just the way you are, because I respect your right to be you, your right to be different.

When I like myself, I am willing to select a mate based upon the belief that I am lovable and capable, and that it's OK for me to be with someone who values me. Selection of my mate will not be based on an attempt to find someone like my mother, or like my father, or the opposite of my mother, or the opposite of my father. I will not select an employer who reject me, or who will expect me to run roughshod over everyone else, like my mother or my father did. I will select a partner based upon a common value system that involves caring for each other. I will select someone who will be open to our sharing thoughts and feelings.

In my quest for intimacy, I will not engage in extremes of selfishness or selflessness. I again remember Rabbi Hillel's words when he said, "If I am not for myself, who will be for me? If I am only for myself, what am I? And if not now, when?" In a state of intimacy, I care about myself, and I care about the people around me. And, in all circumstances, I can take myself and the other person into consideration regarding what I do.

A major goal of this book is to invite people to be intimate with one another. Some of the concepts that foster intimacy are:

First and foremost,
OWN YOUR OWN FEELING, THINKING
AND BEHAVIOR, AND NO ONE ELSE'S.

Share Natural Child feelings, when your Adult says this makes sense.

Confront people from your Nurturing Parent, Adult, and Natural Child.

Ask for what you want, and expect others to do the same, instead of mind-reading and expecting others to know.

Give people positive strokes for what they do, and just for being themselves.

Take an "I'm OK, you're OK" position.

All people have a need to structure their time. They may do so through withdrawing from others and spending time alone. (People seldom get many strokes when they are spending time in withdrawal.) Or they may take part in ritualistic interchanges they were taught during childhood, by following the "proper" formulas for greeting, eating, courting, mourning, worshipping, and so on. (A few strokes here.) They may engage in activities with others—work, hobbies, games, and so on. (Level of stroking increases.) They may choose to engage in what Berne called semi-ritualistic topical conversations with others: pastimes. (Even more strokes.) Or they may take part in psychological games. (The strokes increase in number and intensity.) Of the six ways of structuring time, intimacy provides the highest level of positive stroking. For some people, it also poses the greatest sense of risk. People who are not sure of their own OK-ness often try to find OK-ness through their relationships with others. Because their sense of OK-ness is tentative and is based upon the approval of another person, they have an exaggerated fear of possible negative strokes in intimacy and also fear loss of the positive strokes. They therefore seek intimacy but at the same time consider it to be a high-risk situation.

On the other hand, the risks of intimacy are quite low for people who have accepted themselves. If you like yourself, you can enjoy intimacy and the many positive, unconditional strokes it brings. You will not risk your own OK-ness—if people don't like you, or don't like what you do, or don't want to do what you ask, you are still OK.

There is a place for all the ways of structuring time. I do not want to be intimate with everybody I meet, nor do I wish to spend all my time being intimate with one person. I do not wish to share my feelings all day long with anyone. I want at times to engage in pastimes, to participate in activities together, to do my own thing away from my intimate friend, and so on. Intimacy is not symbiosis. We can be separate and independent, together.

What is symbiosis?

In nature, a number of pairs of different organisms live together in symbiosis, a relationship of mutual dependency. An example of a symbiotic relationship is the hippopotamus with a tick bird on its back: the tick bird needs the hippopotamus to supply ticks for him to eat, and the hippopotamus needs the tick bird to rid him of ticks. Symbiosis is also present in human relationships, as a mutual dependence in which one person has a need to parent and the other person has a need to be parented. A mother and her infant are symbiotic in a healthy way—they must be if the infant is to survive. She feels a strong need to care for her baby and derives pleasure from doing so. The infant truly does *need* to be taken care of, since he is not yet capable of taking care of himself. Symbiosis is therefore a normal developmental stage in infancy. If all goes well, the child takes more and more responsibility for his own well-being until the symbiosis is broken. If the symbiotic relationship persists beyond the age of 2½, however, it can become increasingly crippling and uncomfortable because the child does not learn to function independently and needs to be attached to somebody in order to feel like a whole person. These attachments are usually of an unhealthy nature.

The Schiffs use the word "symbiosis" to describe a certain type of unhealthy relationship in which two individuals are inappropriately dependent upon each other.[31] In this kind of symbiotic relationship, one person uses his Adult (mind-reads, often inaccurately) to figure

149

out what he *thinks* the other person feels, wants and needs or how that person will respond. He then parents the other person, based on that assessment. Meanwhile, Person #2 is in Child and does not use his Adult or Parent. Their transactions are strictly between Parent and Child. In a few minutes, they may very well reverse positions, with Person #2 using his Parent or Adult and Person #1 using only his Child. Though the roles are reversed, the transactions still take place between one person's Parent and the other person's Child. There are no transactions between Parent and Parent, Adult and Adult, or Child and Child because people in symbiosis do not use the same ego states at the same time. They therefore have great difficulty in maintaining OK, complementary transactions. Their Parent-to-Child transactions are primarily from Adapted Child and Critical Parent. It is difficult for them to think together effectively, or to have fun together.

In a symbiotic relationship, only one complete personality is operating at a given time; the two have literally "become one" by giving up use of parts of their personalities. The ego states are divided between the two people, so that if one has access to a certain ego state the other does not. A common division of the ego states is for one person to have use of Critical Parent, Adult, and Natural Child, and the other to have use of Nurturing Parent and Adapted Child, with Little Professor substituting for Adult:

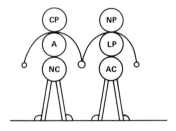

Together, these two people make up one complete personality. They "need" each other because they are halves of a whole.

Is that why we call a spouse "my better half?"

Unfortunately, that may be so. Our culture has encouraged us to adopt stereotypical male/female roles that lead us to discount some of our ego states, so that many of us are going around looking for our "other halves," the parts of ourselves that we have suppressed or failed to develop. We feel incomplete and "need" someone to "make" us feel whole. It was especially common in this culture to discourage little boys from expressing most feelings and discourage little girls from thinking about most things, so that men were looking for someone else to express their tender feelings and women were looking for someone else to think for them. Instead of learning to use all their own effective ego states, they became symbiotic with others who were able to use the ego states they thought they lacked. These symbiotic relationships, which at first felt comfortable and fulfilling, tended to discourage further growth of the individuals involved and to encourage games between them. Often the "love" soon failed, but the bonds of symbiosis held the couple together in a state of unhealthy dependency.

Are you saying that love is symbiotic?

Love between two individuals with complete personalities need not be symbiotic. "Being in love" as described in myths and fairytales is often symbiotic, however. Such feelings of "love" are intense because there is a sense of completion —He can feel angry for me! She can cry for me! —and so on. When someone doesn't express something he feels, the other person will often express it for him; when one person isn't self-motivating, the other is the initiator, et cetera. Couples often marry because they have decided that they can't live without each other; unfortunately they often soon decide that they can't live *with* each other either, because of the symbiotic behaviors that attracted them to each other in the first place.

In therapy, I place emphasis on the importance of breaking the symbiosis. When only one spouse is cooperating in this effort, the other may become uncomfortable or even enraged. I am reminded of a phone call from the irate wife of a client of mine, at 2 a.m. This little old woman from Little Rock, Arkansas, said, "Ayub?" (Abe). I answered "Yes?" She said, "Sym-bah-oh-sis, sym-BAH-*OH*-sis, that's all Ah evuh heah is SYM—BAH—*OH*—SIS!" She then slammed down the receiver. Although I was a little amused, at the same time I sympathized with the fear underlying her anger. Clearly she was seeing her husband's therapy as a threat to the stability of their "close" but unhappy relationship.

Many people are unwilling to disturb the balance of their symbiotic relationships, which may be miserable but nevertheless are both binding and familiar. Growth and change are seen as threats to this type of relationship. Both parties must maintain their old roles, positions, attitudes and behaviors if the symbiosis is to continue, yet doing so often becomes increasingly uncomfortable. *Someone has to be not-OK* for a symbiosis to continue. When one spouse gives up symbiotic behaviors and the other does not, the offended party may very well go and look for somebody else to be symbiotic with (i.e., same marriage all over again), while the spouse who has changed may go to find someone to be autonomous with. When both are willing to give up symbiotic behaviors, they can learn to be autonomous with each other.

Why haven't all of us succeeded in breaking the symbiosis of infancy?

People remain symbiotic from childhood through adulthood because their needs and wants were not met from an OK position in their first thirty months of life. They may have been rejected, neglected, mistreated, parented inappropriately, or separated from their parents. Their parents may have responded to autonomous behavior with anger or fear. For any number of reasons, a symbiotic person has learned, from infancy, that the way to survive is to turn off his own needs and wants in order not to be rejected or harmed by his parents. He has learned how to discount himself. He may have learned that when he has needs the other person must discount her own needs. He has also learned that only one want can be filled at a time: it's either my want or your want. Somebody wins, and somebody loses. The baby learns that he is not OK because he does not have the right to have needs and wants. He has also learned how to "read minds." He tries to figure out what Mama is going to do, what she wants, and what she expects. Through attempted mind-reading, he tries to take care of Mama so that she will take care of him. He may have learned not to cry, to survive without being touched, to rebel, not to express feelings, not to pay attention to pain or hunger. Later on, he learns to relate to others by using the same mechanisms and thought patterns, and by making demands on others the way his parents made demands on him. He still believes that if somebody wins, somebody loses. He still thinks that only one want can be filled at a time. He still feels that it's not OK for people to have needs and wants. And he believes that anybody who really cared about him would read *his* mind and figure out how to take care of him or what he needs and wants.

In a normal symbiosis, the infant sends stimuli to the mother's Parent. Mother, in turn, figures out with her Adult what the baby needs and takes care of the baby with her Parent. Mother will do this even though she may have Child needs and wants of her own; for example, she may need to go to the bathroom but will hold it in until the baby is fed. If she needs a good night's sleep she will nevertheless sleep very lightly "in case the baby cries." To a certain extent, she discounts her own Child needs in favor of the baby's. If this is carried to extremes, the baby may have trouble learning to delay gratification while mom takes care of her own needs. Good parenting requires adequate gratification along with enough appropriate frustration to allow the child to develop his own resources. Certain needs and wants MUST be met, and promptly, if the child is to develop normally. On the other hand, the mother needs to appropriately and gradually balance out her own wants and her child's wants so that neither is discounted and both get their needs met. This helps the youngster learn to delay gratification somewhat and is also helpful in resolving the symbiosis at the appropriate time. If the mother does not do this, she is left with a ten-year-old who makes disturbances while she is trying to talk on the phone, or a 13-year-old who expects her to get up off her sickbed to make dinner, or a four-year-old who has tantrums in the supermarket, or a six-year-old who keeps her at home because he has burned out all the babysitters in the neighborhood. If she discounts her own Natural Child too much while her baby is small, he will see to it that she continues to discount her Natural Child when he is older. If she discounts the baby's Natural Child when he is small, he will learn how to take care of her instead of how to take care of himself.

When symbiosis between mother and child is not successful, the baby does not get his needs and wants met. The mother's Child communicates to the baby's Adult (Little Professor) that she cannot stand the baby having needs and wants and exhibiting certain kinds of behaviors (e.g., the baby sucks too hard, his bowel movements are too smelly, he cries, he is too rambunctious). In response, the baby intuits with his Little Professor that he will not be loved or taken care of if he continues those expressions of his Natural Child. He therefore takes care of Mother's wants by discounting his Natural Child expressions: he stops crying, moving, sucking, etc., in order to get taken care of, if not loved. The symbiosis is reversed: despite limited resources, he is now attempting to take care of Mother in the hope that this will allow him to survive. By not subjecting Mother to things she "can't stand," he hopes to keep her in good enough shape to take care of him. In essence, he has learned that babies are in this world to take care of their mothers.

How can I tell whether my relationships are symbiotic?

If you are in a relationship in which you seem to be taking care of the other person, or criticizing the other person frequently, it's likely that relationship is symbiotic. If you are regularly in need of caretaking, feel dependent, and want the other person to decide things for you and tell you what to do, that also indicates a symbiotic relationship. People in symbiotic relationships believe that they know what the other person is thinking, feeling, or wanting. They often expect the other person to know what they want, or feel, or think. Typically, they say (or think), "If you really loved me, you would have known how I felt and what I wanted." Or, "A really sensitive, caring person would have understood what I needed."

In a symbiosis, feelings and behaviors are often "divided up" so that what one person has the other does not. For example, when a situation calls for one person to feel angry or sad, he may not express it; the other person feels and expresses it for him. Or, only one of them may be angry at a given time. Symbiotic couples tend not to be competent in the same areas: If one is a good cook, the other may not even try to boil water.

In your relationship, if it always appears that both of you can't have what you want and someone must sacrifice, you are probably being symbiotic. Does it appear that one of you usually has to feel "down and out" or that it is not all right for both of you to be happy at the same time? If so, you are probably symbiotic. If you feel that you need someone to complete you or make you a whole person, you are a candidate for a symbiotic relationship.

Are people symbiotic only in close personal relationships?

Symbiotic behaviors are by no means confined to primary relationships. People can be symbiotic in any personal or professional relationship. This often begins with a discount that involves mindreading. One person guesses, or thinks that she knows, what the other person is thinking or feeling, or what the other person will think, feel, or do if she exhibits some behavior. For example, a supervisee may fail to confront a supervisor because she is afraid that he will reject her or get angry at her if she does so. If this fear is based upon past experience, her assessment may be accurate and healthy. If it is only through mind-reading that she "knows" he'll get angry, her failure to make an appropriate confrontation is unhealthy. Not only is she repeating self-discounting behavior she learned as an infant, when she tried to guess what her mother's reactions would be, she is also discounting the other person with her mind-reading.

How often have you been unwilling to dress a certain way, or to say what you thought or felt, because of what you *guessed* the other person would do in response? And how often have you done something you just *assumed* that someone else wanted you to do, without checking this out? It is not uncommon for people to put a lot of energy into doing some unnoticed, unappreciated, or even unwanted thing for someone else. An extreme example of this came to light in a recent marital counseling session, after which the astonished woman turned to her husband and exclaimed, "You mean that I've been doing that for twenty years and you didn't *want* me to?"

In the business world, symbiosis often takes the form of what Dr. Ken Blanchard refers to as "bicycle management." In bicycle management, the supervisor looks like he's riding a bike because he continually kowtows to his superiors (board of directors, customers, supervisor) while stepping on his subordinates. In TA terms, when he is with a customer, his boss, or a member of the board, he tends to be in Compliant Child; that is, he quits thinking, he smiles a lot, and he appears to be bowing because he is continually nodding his head in agreement. His boss tends to be in Parent and to relate to his subordinate's Child. (This is often true of the subsidiary company in its dealings with the parent company.) When the supervisor deals with his own subordinates, however, the symbiosis is reversed: He goes into Parent and relates to their Child ego states. In such a system, it is rare for supervisors and subordinates to use Adult-to-Adult transactions for solving problems. Their transactions are Parent-to-Child and Child-to-Parent, with lots of Adult mind-reading. Here's why:

155

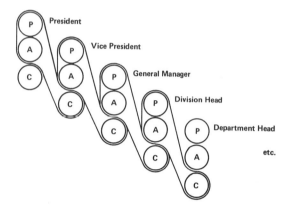

As you can see, this hierarchical symbiosis is a very unhealthy situation. Adult-to-Adult transfers of information do not take place across the various levels of this hierarchy; Adult information does not come up, and what does come down is directed to the recipient's Child. Child-to-Child anger, fun and creativity are similarly blocked. While some Nurturing Parent activity may take place, it moves in only one direction: downward. The person in top-level management is likely to get little or no nurturing for his Child, nor does he believe that he needs it, and there is no one with whom he can relate closely. In such a system, the Parent involved is likely to be Critical; the Child response is therefore often overtly or covertly Rebellious. In short, it's a difficult situation in which everyone is discounting and being discounted.

Another example of symbiosis within an organization occurs when someone believes that she is responsible for the motivation of her subordinates. Such a person in fact believes that she is responsible for whatever doesn't go well and for the resolution of those problems, all by herself. Her department's or company's problem is *her* fault, and she feels solely responsible for solving it. She may even believe that she is responsible for other people's feelings, problem-solving abilities, and competence on the job. People like this need not continue those Parent-Child transactions. They will do much better when they invite their subordinates to examine the facts and problem-solve with them, and when they establish similar relationships with their own supervisors.

How can I stop being symbiotic?

To resolve a symbiosis, get OK, complementary transactions, especially those in which you and the other person are in the same ego state. It is effective crossing of transactions that breaks the symbiosis. In a healthy relationship, I can be in Child while you're in Child and in Adult while you're in Adult, and we can transact Parent-to-Child without one of us being in a not-OK position. Then I can function from all of my ego states, and you can function from all of yours. Each of us will function as a whole person.

Many of the concepts dealt with in this book are ways of helping people break up symbiotic relationships and become autonomous human beings. Perhaps the single most important way of doing this is to avoid discounting. Just as games cannot exist without discounting, symbiosis cannot exist without discounting. If I don't discount myself or you, we will not be symbiotic.

Chapter XI

WHERE DO WE GO FROM HERE?

Now that I've finished this book, I've decided that I want to make some changes. How do I begin?

First, you can review Chapter VI, which gave specific concepts that are extremely helpful in changing behavior. Second, you can keep in mind that the key to change is *action*. Many people spend long hours in planning, figuring out what they want to change and how they could change it. All too frequently, however, they stop short of actually making the changes. You can avoid that pitfall by making a behavioral change *today, now*. It is not necessary for the change to be difficult or dramatic. As I have pointed out many times, a simple change in the language you use can lead to changes in your feelings and in your other behaviors as well. You can pay attention to your ego states and practice switching ego states when the one you're in is not effective in handling the present situation. Each day you can make decisions, both large and small, that reflect a belief that you are OK and so is everyone else. As you model OK-ness, day in and day out, you invite others to change their behaviors as well. As they respond to your OK-ness, you will respond to theirs, so that the "I'm OK, You're OK" position is increasingly reinforced and strengthened, communication improves, and changing becomes easier and easier.

I've been trying hard to change my behavior, but I keep falling back into my old patterns. What's wrong?

A person who has made a script redecision finds it relatively easy to model OK-ness and to change in the here-and-now, as described above. Great difficulty in changing certain behaviors indicates that the person is blocking himself with unfinished business from earlier times in his life. Fritz Perls said that people need to complete unfinished experiences before they can make the changes they need to make and live in the here-and-now. Old, unresolved feelings —often relating to parents or other important people—tend to distort our view of facts here and now. (Remember the transference transactions!) Individuals who are viewing the world through the distorting lenses of unfinished experience may need to make major script redecisions and to have support in doing so. If you are finding it difficult to change your behavior, you could benefit greatly from psychotherapy.

But there's nothing wrong with me! I've never had any major problems in my life, and I've never felt even a little bit crazy. What would therapy do for me?

You don't have to have anything "wrong with you" to benefit from therapy. You don't have to be unhappy or troubled, either. At one time, therapy was supposed to be for people who were miserable, "crazy," or "not OK," just as doctors were supposed to be for people who were gravely ill or badly injured. Now, healthy people go to doctors in order to maintain and improve their physical well-being. Likewise, perfectly sane and "normal" people go to psychotherapists. Therapy is like a mirror in which they can see their own behavior more clearly, as well as the behavior of others. In therapy, they can get practice and support in changing their behavior, and feedback that helps confirm and reinforce those changes.

If I wanted to remodel my house, I *could* do it all by myself, but it would certainly be a difficult task. It would also take me quite a long time. I'm not a carpenter, a plumber, a mason, or an electrician, so I would have a lot to learn by experience. If the time it took didn't matter to me, and if I were willing to put a lot of extra energy into the job, I'd eventually get the house into pretty good shape. If time did matter to me, however, or if I needed my energy for other things, it would make sense for me to get some expert help with the remodeling. The expert might even have some good ideas that had never occurred to me, and the results of my remodeling project might be more gratifying than I had expected. It is the same when remodeling my behavior: I can do it myself, and it's easier with some competent help.

Accepting the benefits of therapy is especially difficult for people who are trying to maintain a Be Strong or macho image. They think it isn't OK to get help. They'd rather stay stuck, or try to muddle through, and the results are often unfortunate or even tragic. If they're miserable enough, they might see a shrink but not want to admit it. Actually, when a person admits that he wants and gets an objective source of feedback and support, he is admitting to his own OK-ness. He is admitting that he values himself and his relationships with others, and that he is willing to learn and change. My own therapy was an affirmation of my OK-ness and an important turning point in my life. Thousands of other mentally healthy people have had similar experiences with therapy.

I think I could use some therapy, but won't other people think this is an admission of craziness or weakness?

Therapy is now widely understood as a road to personal growth. Unfortunately, however, some people still do attach a stigma to psychotherapy. Often these are the very people who could most benefit from therapy themselves, if they were willing to take advantage of it. Those who think that strong, normal, healthy people never need therapy are simply misinformed. They do not know what therapy has to offer today. As more and more people give credit to the part psychotherapy has played in their attaining increased creativity, productivity, contentment and joy, fewer and fewer will think of therapy as "head-shrinking" performed by a witch doctor with a Viennese accent. Therapy is actually a process of *expansion*—of increasing awareness, expanding options, and growing skills in communication. It can be the beginning of a fascinating journey of exploration and learning, in which you set out with a guide and later continue by yourself as a seasoned traveler.

How do I know if I need therapy?

One good indication of the need for therapy is that an "I'm not OK" or "You're not OK" position is predominant in your life. Do you *really* think you're OK, most of the time? Can you honestly say that you believe other people are also OK, most of the time? If not, you have made decisions that it would be well to examine in therapy. Another indication of the need for therapy is that you have been "trying" to change some significant behavior or behaviors but have not been successful in doing so. Do the same unfortunate things keep happening over and over again? Do you feel like a loser or a failure? Do you have trouble with your relationships? A simple question to ask yourself is, "Do I feel happy?"

Where do I go for therapy?

In almost all urban areas in this country, both public and private facilities are available. A friend who has had a successful experience in therapy can be a good source of information. Your family physician is another. I urge you to consider doing your own interviewing when hiring a therapist, and to inquire as to her or his educational credentials. In general, social workers and psychiatric nurses with masters degrees, psychologists with Ph.D.'s, and psychiatrists, who have M.D.'s, have the necessary educational background. Many

161

professional organizations have further requirements for credentialing which they deem advisable; you might therefore check with the professional organizations representing the therapists you have in mind. Additionally, many states attempt to ensure high quality in psychotherapy through licensing laws. Licensure by the state is further indication that a person is a qualified therapist.

The International Transactional Analysis Association, through approved training programs and a system of written and oral examinations, grants certification to people who are proficient in TA, as Clinical Members or Teaching Members. (The ITAA also grants Special Fields certification to educators, consultants, and others who are not psychotherapists but who use TA in their fields of expertise.) If you want to know the ITAA membership status of anyone who presents himself as a TA therapist, or if you want to find a TA therapist in your area, you can get information by writing to:

> The International Transactional Analysis
> Association, Inc.
> 1772 Vallejo Street
> San Francisco, California 94123

Needless to say, educational and legal credentials do not necessarily indicate that a person is a capable, competent psychotherapist. Also, a few fine therapists may be found who have rather unimpressive credentials, though this selection is risky. In your interviewing process, you'll need to use both your Adult and Little Professor to assess how "together" that therapist is. Does the therapist model the kinds of behaviors that he or she talks about, and that you might wish to emulate? Does the therapist appear to be interested in you, to be objective, to be appropriately nurturing instead of Rescuing? Are there people you can check with to find out their experience with this therapist? Ultimately, your own intuitive sense is likely to be the best measure of a therapist's capabilities.

What happens in therapy?

Each therapist has her or his own personal style and preferred techniques. It would be hard to say "what happens" because the content of the sessions is directly related to the mode of treatment used and the personality of the therapist. Even within the realm of a single school of psychotherapy like Transactional Analysis, for example, the therapist may be active or relatively inactive. It is likely that a TA therapist will prefer group therapy, although she may also do individual therapy. My own preference, and the preference of TA therapists in general, is for group therapy. I find it to be more efficient and more effective. Perhaps this is because, in group therapy, the therapist sees you "in life." A group is a sort of laboratory where you deal with people of the same sex and of the opposite sex, younger and older, who leave and enter the group. As you change your behavior in the group, you change it outside the group as well. Group support provides a very powerful kind of permission, and feedback from an entire group often has a great deal more impact than feedback from a single individual would have.

Such issues as contaminations, transferences, destructive Parent messages, "I'm not OK" and "You're not OK" behaviors, are but a few of the items that may be addressed in TA and other forms of psychotherapy. As these issues are dealt with, people learn to cope effectively with everyday feelings, conflicts, and stress.

I don't want to get dependent on a therapist, or stay in therapy for years. Isn't that a danger?

Some people fear therapy because they believe that it is a crutch that will make them become dependent on their therapist. A good therapist will not tell you what to do, will not think for you, and will not feel for you. Instead, you will be invited to do your own thinking, feel your own feelings, and make your own decisions. Even when you're in therapy, you're doing the work yourself. If a therapist Rescues you, then I invite you to reconsider your selection.

In TA, therapy is "by contract." In other words, you decide what you want to accomplish, and your therapist agrees to assist you in reaching that goal. When your goal is reached, the contract is complete; you have both done what you agreed to do. You can leave therapy at that point, or you can decide to make a contract to accomplish something else. At any rate, your therapy has clearly defined goals, set by you, and you will know when you have reached them. Effective therapy is not a never-ending search for OK-ness or enlightenment. Rather than making you more dependent, it increases your independence and autonomy. You will know when you have gotten what you need and want from therapy, and you may be surprised at how quickly you reach your goals.

What does the therapist do to help me reach my goals?

The psychotherapist provides potency, permission and protection. When the client trusts the therapist, he sees the therapist as more potent than the Parent in his head that is sending him those "not-OK" messages. Because the therapist is more powerful than the troublesome Parent, the client begins to listen instead to the therapist, who provides many kinds of permissions. Permissions are messages that "it's OK to ..." or "you don't have to ...." The therapist provides permissions by modeling as well as in words. With the therapist's permission and potency, the client is willing to change some of the behaviors he has been unwilling to change in the past. He will often then need the protection of the therapist and/or the group to ward off the destructive Parent messages that he will hear when he changes behaviors, as well as to cope with the guilt and fear which often accompany going against old Parent messages. After a while, the client finds that the terrible things his Child believed would happen if he showed feelings, or asked for what he wanted, or confronted other people's not-OK behavior, or enjoyed himself, rarely occur. Simultaneously, he begins to incorporate into his own personality the Nurturing Parent messages he is receiving. Then the amount of energy he puts into Adapted Child and Critical Parent diminishes and, for all practical purposes, he is finished with therapy.

How can I incorporate TA within my organization?

Essential to any change is a willingness on the part of key people to look at themselves and their organization from an I'm OK-You're OK position. Unfortuantely, executives often do not understand the importance of "people skills," which are necessary for continued growth and well-being of the organization. Too frequently, key personnel tend to feel threatened by the idea of looking at their own behaviors. It often helps to bring in an outside consultant who can provide permission, protection and potency for these people within a TA training program.

How do we find a consultant?

Information about TA consultants is also available through the ITAA. A number of individuals have a variety of programs available that can be tailored to meet the needs of your organization.

If your organization is in need of a top-notch consultant, who should I recommend? Me, of course!

Abe Wagner
Transactional Analysis Communications, Inc.
2755 South Locust, #101
Denver, Colorado, 80222
(303) 757-7576

Whether you decide to utilize a therapist or consultant in learning how to apply the information in this book, or decide to do it yourself, I believe that thoughtful use of these concepts will significantly improve the quality of your life, at home as well as at work.

QUALITIES OF EFFECTIVE MANAGERS

A. They have a positive self-image. They are self-confident.

B. They have a positive attitude about others. They view all people as having inherent worth and dignity.

C. They have the technical knowledge needed to get the job done well.

D. They are well organized and take a planful approach to work.

E. They are good teachers and effective communicators.

F. They are appropriately assertive. They are willing to persevere and to go after what they want.

G. They have reasonable and consistent expectations. They can be flexible when flexibility is appropriate.

H. They are confrontive in a sensitive way. They are firm with peers, subordinates and supervisors when the situation calls for firmness.

I. They are willing to express their "mads" as well as their "glads."

J. They are empathetic, understanding and supportive.

K. They give positive strokes to subordinates, peers, and their supervisors.

L. They will admit to their own "resistable" behavior, and their own errors in judgment. They are willing to say "I'm sorry" or "I apologize."

M. They are willing to admit to not knowing the answer.

N. They vary their style of leadership, depending on the maturity of their subordinates. They know how to use both a "telling" style and a "delegating" style.

O. They involve their peers and subordinates in decision-making and in assumption of responsibility.

It is rare for one person to possess all of these qualities. Effective managers continue to increase their skills in these areas.

YOU ARE SIX DIFFERENT PEOPLE

A. The people in your head, and in mine, have six different personalities (ego states). Three of these are effective in almost all situations, and three of these are ineffective in almost all situations.

B. The effective ego states are:

1. *The Natural Child*

   a. It has needs for strokes, structure, recognition, and stimulation.

   b. It has wants which vary from moment to moment.

   c. If needs and wants are met, it expresses warmth.
   If needs and wants are not met, it expresses anger, sadness, and fear.

   d. The Natural Child looks like, sounds like, and is in fact a spontaneous little kid experiencing these needs, wants, and feelings.

2. *The Adult*

   a. It is like a computer that takes in, stores, processes, and sends out information.

   b. It is logical, reasonable, and rational.

   c. It deals with facts and thinking instead of feelings, attitudes, and opinions.

   d. It is the part of you that is used to determine whether, when, and how to express yourself.

3. *The Nurturing Parent*

   a. It is empathetic and understanding.

   b. It is sensitive to the needs, wants, and feelings of others.

   c. It is firm in a caring and non-demanding way.

C. The ineffective ego states are:

1. *The Critical Parent*

   a. It communicates that you are not okay by words, gestures, facial expressions, body posture, and/or tone of voice.

   b. It often points a finger and speaks louder.

   c. It is sometimes sarcastic.

2. *The Rebellious Child*

   a. It says that it's not going to listen to you, agree with you, or do what you want.

   b. It tends to get angrier than the situation calls for, and it stays angry longer.

   c. It is very negative. This may be obvious or subtle.

   d. It rebels indirectly by forgetting, procrastinating, and doing things differently, half-way, or poorly.

3. *The Compliant Child*

   a. It communicates "I'm not okay" in subtle (or not-so-subtle) ways.

   b. It speaks with a softer voice, uses wishy-washy words, and rarely makes eye contact. It tends to whine.

   c. Its behavior is to be very careful and self-protective.

D. The key is to activate the three effective ego states as much as possible, and to deactivate the ineffective ego states as much as possible.

E. To activate the three effective ego states in your head, do any of the following:

1. Talk to yourself—out loud if alone, or in your head if not alone.

170

a. Nurture yourself, (that is, be kind to yourself), understand your own feelings, be empathetic; give yourself a pep talk.

b. Be logical. Ask yourself specific questions regarding the feelings or attitudes that you are experiencing, to determine their validity or invalidity.

c. Fantasize about things you like to do or about places you'd like to be.

d. Be unceasingly positive in the face of reasonable negatives, and do this firmly—ten positives for every negative thought or feeling.

2. Practice rehearsing a scene, in your head, about a particular situation in which you wish to succeed. Make this rehearsal real—see it, hear it, feel it. Rehearse regularly until you feel comfortable and competent to handle the actual situation. Such rehearsals will help you to be successful automatically.

F. When other people are in ineffective ego states, stimulate their Natural Child, or Adult, or Nurturing Parent by relating to them from your Nurturing Parent, Adult, and Natural Child.

G. Effective communication takes place when your Nurturing Parent, Adult, and Natural Child relate to the other person's Nurturing Parent, Adult, and Natural Child.

1. Adult-to-Adult transactions are needed for problem-solving, determining probabilities, and exchanging data and information.

2. Natural Child-to-Natural Child transactions are needed for intimacy; that is, for sharing feelings in an authentic and sensitive way.

3. Natural Child-to-Nurturing Parent stimuli are needed to elicit assistance, understanding, empathy, or comforting.

4. Nurturing Parent-to-Natural Child stimuli are needed for providing direction, caring, understanding, and firmness.

5. Nurturing Parent-to-Nurturing Parent transactions are useful for making favorable comments about a third party or deciding how to nurture that person.

CHECKPOINTS FOR HIRING

A. *Does the applicant have all the skills necessary for doing this job well?*

Avoid making assumptions about a person's capabilities — check them out. The "Peter Principle" is often borne out when it is simply *assumed* that, for example, anyone who is technically competent will also have good "people skills."

B. *Have I checked with the applicant?*

What does he think and feel about taking on this job? Ask! Make sure the person *wants* the job and that it *makes sense* to him to have the job.

C. *Does he know what the job entails?*

Let the applicant see an accurate job description before asking him whether he wants to accept the position.

D. *Have I paid attention to my intuition?*

Is there agreement between the verbal information you have about the applicant (references, education, experience, what he says to you) and the non-verbal information you have received? Do you have a "gut-level feeling" that he's the person for the job?

E. *Have I made good use of his references?*

Contact the references and ask questions that invite them to "level" with you, such as: "If you were in my place, would you hire him?"

TWO MAY BE TOO MANY BOSSES

A. Supervision is best done by following "lines of authority."

B. Suggest that there be a working agreement to cross lines of authority, with the understanding that this is done when the person's supervisor is unavailable and the circumstances warrant it.

C. Going to someone else's employee, or over someone's head, leads to unnecessary difficulties.

D. Part of delegating responsibility is granting the authority necesary to carry it out. An employee's authority needs to match his responsibilities.

E. When people are ready, delegate authority.

F. Effective supervisors provide the direction and support to help people grow. Groom people to be able to take your place should the need arise. This does not endanger your job; in fact, it can facilitate your own promotion.

RESPONSIBILITY WITH AUTHORITY

A. Allow a person to read his job description before agreeing to take on the job.

B. A job description is a useful guideline and does not need to be a "straitjacket."

C. Job descriptions may include a description of a job in specific terms, hours, supervision information, etc.

D. Job descriptions may be changed by mutual agreement.

E. People function best when they are clear about their responsibility and their authority.

F. Be specific about what decisions a person may make independently and what decisions will require the supervisor's feedback and / or approval.

G. Make certain that you delegate the authority needed to carry out the responsibility.

H. Before delegating a responsibility, make sure that the person is capable of assuming it.

I. After people assume new responsibilities, provide whatever support they need—extra time with the boss and others, supportive information and feedback, etc.

STRUCTURE FOR SUCCESS

A. People need this kind of clarity to function effectively and comfortably on the job.

B. Job descriptions, written policies, lines of authority, parameters of authority, and decision-making policies help people to function well.

C. Inconsistent application of the above is often destructive.

D. It is vital that people be held accountable for their behavior. If this is inconsistent or nonexistent, many people—and perhaps the whole organization—may flounder.

E. A regular schedule for one-to-one supervisory sessions (perhaps weekly or monthly) is very useful because it shows the supervisee that you care, and it gives both of you the opportunity to plan for the meeting. If sessions are not scheduled regularly, it often happens that "we don't find the time to do it."

F. A key to making things happen is to define the *who, what, when, where, how,* and *why.*

G. *Structure and strokes* are a powerful combination. Together, they can ensure a program's success.

MAKE CONTRACTS AND KEEP THEM

A. Contracts are agreements. These agreements represent your "word," your "character," so abide by them.

B. Your *first* contract is primary (e.g., to be home for dinner at 6 p.m. or to get a piece of work done at a certain time) and is best seen as something to be honored. Avoid changing contracts whenever feasible.

C. If an agreement needs to be changed (for example, if keeping your contract to complete a certain piece of work means that you cannot keep your contract to be home at 6 o'clock), make sure you contact the person with whom you have the agreement and negotiate a different contract (e.g., "Shall I call you when I'm finished? Or would you rather meet me here and go out for dinner?").

D. If people break their contracts with you, confront this. If you don't, you contribute to the breakdown of future contracts with them and to the invalidation of contracts in general.

E. Often, agreeements are made when a person really doesn't want to do what he is contracting to do but is reluctant to say so. Such contracts are often broken "unintentionally." If you don't want to make an agreement, speak up—in a sensitive way. If the other person seems reluctant to make the contract, encourage him to voice his objections. Usually a compromise agreement can be reached that will satisfy both of you and that really will be carried out.

F. Two supervisors often give conflicting directives or give work that conflicts with a schedule that has already been agreed upon. When this occurs, point it out (e.g., "I've already told Tom I'd have his work done by tomorrow"). If he insists, invite him to talk to the other person.

G. You can contract to ask someone something or to point something out. (For example, "I have a strong feeling about something, and I'd like to tell you about it. Would you be up for listening to me?")

H. When making an agreement or asking for something, make sure that you clearly define what you want. (For example, if you want understanding when talking about your "bad day" at the office, ask for it—otherwise, you may end up getting advice instead of understanding.)

I. Contract with your supervisee to help make the supervisory session a "give and take," and expect him to prepare for the session.

J. Contract for "no discounting" and set aside time to "level" at each session. During leveling time, both of you are free to share positive and negative (constructive criticism) strokes.

GUIDELINES FOR MAKING AND
TRANSMITTING DECISIONS

A. If decisions will affect others, it makes sense to involve them in the decision-making process.

B. When people are involved in making a decision, they will be more likely to see that it is implemented (and vice versa).

C. When new ideas or decisions are announced, expect "paranoia" (e.g., "What's she up to?") and resistance ("The old way is better," "I don't want to," et cetera).

D. If you give a person the responsibility to make a decision, accept his decision and back him up. If you aren't prepared to do this, don't give him that responsibility.

E. *Flexibility* is willingness to change a decision if new information indicates that a change is warranted.

F. *Consistency* is to stick by the original decision as long as new information doesn't warrant a change.

G. *Inconsistency* is to change (or fail to stand by) the original decision without sound reason.

H. When decisions are made and new information is available, pass it on as soon as it is feasible to do so.

I. Useful ways of communicating information include regularly scheduled management meetings and memos automatically sent to those who are affected by the decisions.

J. To put decisions into action, provide structure; that is, make it clear who will do what, by when, and so on.

WORDS MAKE A DIFFERENCE

A. Sometimes, your choice of words will determine how your message is received.

B. Avoid asking questions as a way of putting in your opinion (e.g., "Don't you think we should...?"). When you have a point of view, take responsibility for it by making a direct statement (e.g., "I think it would be a good idea to...").

C. Questions with *who, when, how,* etc., are better than questions about *why:* "What are the reasons you were late?"

D. Say *I* when you mean *I,* instead of saying *we, people, one, they,* etc.

E. *Can'ts* and *have to's* are rarely accurate. It is often better to use "I'd rather not," "I'm not up for doing that," "I'd prefer to do this instead," and so on.

F. Avoid exaggerations such as *everybody, nobody, always,* and *never.*

G. *And* is better than *but*; e.g., "You do a good job, *and* lately you've been missing some deadlines." (The word "but" negates whatever precedes it.)

H. To *try* is usually ineffective. Agreements to "do" are better than agreements to "try." *Do it* instead of *trying to do it.*

KEYS TO RUNNING A SUCCESSFUL MEETING

A. These ideas can be applied to almost any type of meeting (management, sales, board of directors, etc).

B. Make certain that several people are involved in planning the agenda. Ask for input from others.

C. During the meeting, involve others as much as possible in planning, decision-making, assumption of responsibility, and cross-communication. Make sure that opportunities for involvement in these areas are included in the agenda.

D. Meeting time is an excellent time for people to share appreciations and to let others know about things they have accomplished.

E. It is often a good idea to hold supervisory meetings on a regular schedule, at a specified time. This ensures better preparation and easier attendance, since people know well in advance not to schedule other activities for that time slot. It is easier to cancel a scheduled meeting that is not needed than it is to schedule a meeting that has become urgent. Meetings that do not take place on a regular schedule tend to not take place at all.

F. The most boring meetings tend to focus on report-giving.

CONFRONTATION ISN'T A DIRTY WORD

A. Why confront? To facilitate changes for the better. When people are being ineffective or inefficient, or are discounting you, somebody else, themselves or a problem, caring confrontation invites them to change these behaviors.

B. You may choose not to concern yourself with someone's ineffective behavior. If so, you will not need to confront the person at all.

C. If you say it straight, you are much less likely to show it crooked. Remember that you cannot *really* hide strong feelings successfully.

D. Confrontation is best done on a one-to-one basis, not in front of others.

E. You can contract to confront—for example, "I have some feelings about something you've done. Are you up for lending me an ear?"

F. Confronting people gets the most successful results when people also get positive strokes ("for what you do and for being you"—see "Everybody Wants to Feel Important").

G. Confrontation can be done with a light touch, and can even be playful.

H. Remember that *do's* are better than *don'ts*; e.g., "Don't handle customers that way" vs, "Listen to customers when they complain and let them know that you understand."

I. Pair authentic positives with negatives when giving constructive criticism; for example, "If you had handled that customer the way you usually do, I'd have no complaints."

J. If you're angry, make sure you express this at a time when you're likely to be heard.

K. To handle anger well, follow this pattern: "I tell you how *I* feel, about what *you're* doing, and *I* ask for what I want instead."

L. When a person repeatedly does the same inappropriate or ineffective thing, or appears to have an ongoing detrimental attitude, it is often wise to discuss this with the person. If people don't change their ineffective behaviors, then put more constructive energy into inviting them to change. Remember, people change when they feel *uncomfortable* with their behavior or with people's responses to their behavior. They may not ever become uncomfortable enough to want to make changes unless you are persistent and sensitive in your confrontations. Remember to remain self-confident rather than aggressive, and avoid challenging the person you are confronting. Structure the confrontation so that the person *wins* by changing his behavior.

M. Instead of being "defensive," listen to what others are saying and let them know you are getting their messages. While listening, it sometimes helps to ask questions that the other person must *think about* in order to answer. After you understand what they are saying, ask yourself, "How can we *both* win?"

N. In the face of difficult situations (e.g., when people are drunk, violent, irrational or hysterical), it is helpful to remain self-confident and take charge.

O. When people won't change and you aren't willing to accept this, stop transacting with them. When you do so from an "I'm OK, you're OK" position, without rejecting the person, you leave the door open for future discussion.

EVERYONE WANTS TO FEEL IMPORTANT

A. Remember that strokes (units of attention) are a *need* and that it is all right to want attention.

B. *What you stroke is what you get.* The behavior that is paid attention to is the behavior that will be repeated. ("If the only time my boss or my father notices me is when I do something wrong, then that's what I'll do.")

C. Supervisors tend to give mostly negative strokes, and employees tend not to stroke the boss at all. If such stroking patterns exist within your organization, it's worthwhile to identify and change them. Everyone needs positive strokes, including the boss.

D. "The ordinary leader gets the people to think highly of the leader. The extraordinary leader gets the people to think highly of themselves."

Chris Hagerty, business consultant

E. People benefit from *two kinds* of positive strokes: I stroke you *for what you do* ("You did a nice job on that." "You handled that customer well."); I stroke you *for being you* (e.g., "I like you," "How are you?", a smile, a touch, "Sure, I have time to talk!").

F. People also need *constructive* criticism (see the outline on confrontation).

G. Confront privately. Give positive strokes privately and publicly.

CAN I GO OVER SOMEONE'S HEAD?

A. Handle disagreements directly, as much as it makes sense to do so.

B. See principles on *confrontation.*

C. Make sure that you have clearly examined your own behavior. If you believe "it's all somebody else's fault," you're likely to stay stuck. You owe it to yourself—and to the other person—to pay attention to your timing, the way you request information or help, your method of confrontation, and so on.

D. Sometimes you may decide that the plusses outweigh the minuses and that you can therefore live with and feel okay about your boss's behavior.

E. You may decide to go to your boss's peer to get help and objective feedback, as opposed to "telling on him." It is advisable to let him know beforehand that you're going to do this.

F. If you wish to "go over his head," invite him to go with you so that both of you can get objective feedback.

G. Remember that "going over someone's head" is a last resort. Let him know that you're going and what you plan to say, if he chooses not to go with you.

H. The boss must avoid taking sides. When employees come to you with problems, intervene to help them talk to each other and to resolve the conflict. If you must take a position, do so on the basis of the facts, not on the basis of whose personality you prefer.

I. The boss must handle any third-party complaints objectively and sensitively, after listening to all sides.

PEOPLE'S BEHAVIOR FIRES THEM

A. In good supervision, you have received positive strokes (for what *you do* and for *being you*) and have been given constructive criticism regularly (see "Confrontation").

B. Constructive criticism focuses on clear, specific expectations.

C. A periodic or annual evaluation should be a summary of the pros and cons which have already been clearly discussed.

D. Remember that change rarely happens overnight. Expect to see a pattern of growth with some periodic backsliding.

E. Before deciding to fire someone, let him know that:

1. You are considering this but haven't decided.

2. This decision is really his, because it's his behavior that will fire him or keep him on the job.

3. You want him to decide whether he wants to stay, and show you his decision by what he does, as it is too heavy an issue for you.

4. You're pulling for him to show that it is his decision to stay.

TIPS FOR A HAPPY LIFE

A. Everybody has inherent worth and dignity. Therefore, deal with people in caring and sensitive ways. Appropriate firmness can show respect for their worth as human beings.

B. It's easy to know what's wrong with the other person, but a little harder to realize your own part in the situation. Ask yourself, "How can I change so that I will be more effective in getting the responses I desire?"

C. It's okay to express anger, fear, sadness, and warmth when it makes sense to do so.

D. Take charge of your own thinking, feeling, and behavior, and no one else's. Remember that neither events nor people *make* you feel good or bad (and vice versa). Be in charge of your response to people and events. You can only *invite* people (customers, employees) to be happy—they decide to accept your invitation.

E. Live in the "here and now." Learn from the past, and feel good about the past, but don't beat yourself for past misdeeds. The security of the future lies in the stability of today.

F. Instead of mind-reading, *ask* if you want to know what someone else wants. Rather than trying to figure out what someone else might want, as a basis for your decisions, focus on what *you* want and do what you decide is sensible after taking into account the wants of others.

G. When you decide that you are capable and lovable, you will automatically invite capable and lovable people to interact with you.

REFERENCES

1. Peter, Laurence J., and Hull, Raymond: THE PETER PRINCIPLE. William Morrow, New York, 1969.

2. Berne, Eric: WHAT DO YOU SAY AFTER YOU SAY HELLO? Grove Press, New York, 1972, p. 85.

3. Ibid., p. 418.

4. Steiner, Claude: SCRIPTS PEOPLE LIVE. Grove Press, New York, 1974.

5. Berne, HELLO, p. 11.

6. Penfield, W.: "Memory Mechanisms," *Archives of Neurology and Psychiatry*, 67: 178-198, 1952.

7. Berne, Eric: GAMES PEOPLE PLAY. Grove Press, New York, 1964, p. 14.

8. Levine, S.: "Stimulation in Infancy," *Scientific American*, 202: 80-86, 1960.

9. Schiff, Jacqui: personal communication.

10. Karpman, Stephen B.: "Fairy Tales and Script Drama Analysis," *Transactional Analysis Bulletin*, Vol. 7, No. 26, 1968, p. 39.

11. Spitz, R.: "Hospitalism: Genesis of Psychiatric Conditions in Early Childhood," *Psychoanalytic Study of the Child*, 1: 53-74, 1945.

12. Steiner, Claude: A WARM FUZZY TALE, Jalmar Press, Sacramento, 1977.

13. Goulding, Robert, and Goulding, Mary: "Injunctions, Decisions, and Redecisions," *Transactional Analysis Journal,* 6: 41-48, 1976.

14. Steiner, Claude: SCRIPTS ALCOHOLICS LIVE. Grove Press, 1971.

15. Dusay, John M.: EGOGRAMS. Harper & Row, New York, 1977.

16. Berne, GAMES.

17. Goulding, Robert, and Goulding, Mary: personal communication.

18. Kahler, Taibi: TA REVISITED. Human Development Publications, Little Rock, Ark., 1978, pp. 275-280.

19. Kisling, Jack: "The Unsilent Generation," *The Denver Post,* July 5, 1979.

20. Schiff, Jacqui Lee, Schiff, Aaron W., Mellor, Ken, et al.: CATHEXIS READER: TRANSACTIONAL ANALYSIS TREATMENT OF PSYCHOSIS. Harper & Row, New York, 1975, pp. 14, 20.

21. Ibid., pp. 14-16.

22. Ibid., pp. 54-55.

23. Berne, HELLO, p. 335.

24. Schiff et al., op cit., pp. 73-74.

25. Ibid., p. 20.

26. Ibid., p. 20.

27. Blanck, Gertrude, and Blanck, Rubin: EGO PSYCHOLOGY, Vol. 1. Columbia University Press, New York, 1974, p. 113.

28. Karpman, Stephen B.: in abstracts by Arlie D'Angelo, *Transactional Analysis Journal*, 5: 74, 1975

29. Kahler, Taibi, and Capers, Hedges: "The Miniscript," *Transactional Analysis Journal*, 4: 26, 1974.

30. Wyckoff, Hogie: "Radical Psychotherapy and Transactional Analysis in Women's Groups," *Transactional Analysis Bulletin*, 9: 36, 128-133, October, 1970.

—————. "Banal Scripts of Women," *in* SCRIPTS PEOPLE LIVE, Chapter 14 (Steiner, op. cit.).

31. Schiff et al., op. cit., pp. 5-9.

SUGGESTED READING

These books are available through your bookstore, or through Transactional Publications, P.O. Box 3932 Rincon Annex, San Francisco, CA 94119.

Babcock, Dorothy, and Keepers, Terry: RAISING KIDS OK: TA in Human Growth and Development. Grove Press, New York, 1976.

Berne, Eric: GAMES PEOPLE PLAY. Grove Press, New York, 1964.

Berne, Eric: WHAT DO YOU SAY AFTER YOU SAY HELLO? Grove Press, New York, 1972.

Dusay, John M.: EGOGRAMS. Harper & Row, New York, 1977.

Harris, Thomas A.: I'M OK, YOU'RE OK: A Practical Guide to Transactional Analysis. Harper & Row, New York, 1967.

James, Muriel, and Jongeward, Dorothy: BORN TO WIN: TA with Gestalt Experiments. Addison-Wesley Publishing Company, 1971.

Schiff, Jacqui: ALL MY CHILDREN.

Steiner, Claude: SCRIPTS PEOPLE LIVE: Transactional Analysis of Life Scripts. Grove Press, New York, 1974.

193

195